NEVER THE SINNER

NEVER THE SINNER

the leopold and loeb story

John Logan

THE OVERLOOK PRESS
WOODSTOCK & NEW YORK

First published in the United States in 1999 by
The Overlook Press, Peter Mayer Publishers, Inc.
Lewis Hollow Road
Woodstock, New York 12498

Copyright © 1988 by John Logan

Library of Congress Cataloging-in-Publication Data

Logan, John, 1961–
Never the sinner. : the Leopold and Loeb story / John Logan
p. cm.
1. Leopold, Nathan Freudenthal, 1904 or 5–1971—Drama.
2. Loeb, Richard A., 1905 or 6–1936—Drama. 3. Trials (Murder)—Illinois—
Chicago—Drama. 4. Murderers—Illinois—Chicago—Drama.
I. Title.
PS3562.04472N48   1999
98-47733
812'.54—dc21

Book design and type formatting by Bernard Schleifer
Manufactured in the United States of America
FIRST EDITION
3 5 7 9 8 6 4 2
ISBN 0-87951-930-4

FOR MOLLY HAGAN

"Never growing older, never growing wiser, children ever."

And with thanks to all those who have been instrumental in the development of this play: James Bagley, Donna Powers Branson, Geoff Bullen, Rob Croser, David Downs, Stephen Graham, Ann Hartdegen, Linda Jenkins, Terry McCabe, Ethan McSweeny, Marty Madden, Denis O'Hare, Sir Anthony Quayle, Jeffrey Richards, David Roach, John Swanbeck, and with particular thanks to Elmer Gertz, without whom this play could not have been written.

SETTING

Chicago, Illinois. The summer of 1924.

CAST OF CHARACTERS

LEOPOLD: *Nathan Leopold, Jr. Highly intellectual student. Eighteen years old. Leopold is at once coldly academic and fiercely romantic. He is nervous, arrogant, obsessed, and bird-like.*

LOEB: *Richard Loeb. Another highly intellectual student. Nineteen years old. Amoral, with scary flashes of true madness. Loeb is very attractive and projects an ambiguous sexual appeal and a distinct personal flair. Cat-like.*

CROWE: *Robert Crowe. Pugnacious and severe State's Attorney. He is a slick Chicago lawyer and politician, intelligent and wily.*

DARROW: *Clarence Darrow. Humane, salty, tired, and slouched. An old roaring lion, sixty-seven years old and still fighting.*

REPORTER 1: *Older, seasoned reporter.*
Also plays Dr. White, Sergeant Gortland and Bailiff.

REPORTER 2: *Younger, somewhat jaded reporter.*
Also plays Germaine Rheinhardt and Dr. Hulbert.

REPORTER 3: *Younger, cub reporter.*
Also plays Dr. Bowman.

SET

A very simple, evocative setting to allow for liquid, open staging.

NOTES

The full cast remains on stage for the entire play, watching the action.

As much as possible the scenes should flow effortlessly and quickly from one to the next in a fluid, almost cinematic style.

And one final point to remember: this is a love story.

This version of NEVER THE SINNER premiered in Adelaide, Australia, on August 18, 1994 at the Space Theatre, presented by Independent Theatre. The cast was as follows:

Leopold .... Nicholas Bishop
Loeb .... Russel Bedford
Darrow .... Allen Munn
Crowe .... David Roach
Reporter 1 .... Les Zetlein
Reporter 2 .... Eva Hamburg
Reporter 3 .... Darren Paul

Directed by Rob Croser
Set by Rod Roach
Lighting by Laraine Wheeler

NEVER THE SINNER premiered in 1985 at Stormfield Theatre in Chicago. It was directed by Terry McCabe. The cast was as follows: Denis O'Hare, Bryan Stillman, Richard Brown, Jerome Bloom, Tom Carroll, Donna Powers, and Mitch Webb.

NEVER THE SINNER opened in London at the Playhouse Theatre on March 29, 1990, presented by Diversey Productions. It was directed by Geoff Bullen. The cast was as follows: Denis O'Hare, Ben Daniels, Joss Ackland, Julian Glover, Peter Banks, DeNica Fairman, and Richard Cawte.

NEVER THE SINNER premiered in New York at the Raymond J. Greenwald Theatre on December 1, 1997. The Signature Theatre (Arlington, VA) production was presented by the American Jewish Theatre. It subsequently reopened at the John Houseman Theatre on January 24, 1998. The cast was as follows:

Leopold .... Jason Bowcutt
Loeb .... Michael Solomon
Darrow .... Robert Hogan
Crowe .... Glen Pannell
Reporter 1 .... Paul Mullina
Reporter 2 .... Jurian Hughes
Reporter 3 .... Howard W. Overshown

Directed by Ethan McSweeny
Set by Lou Stanari
Lighting by Howard Binkley

INTRODUCTION
Twenty Years With Leopold and Loeb

THE STORY

IN Chicago, on May 21, 1924, Nathan Leopold Jr. and Richard Loeb killed fourteen-year-old Bobby Franks. Leopold and Loeb were stylish, rich, and hugely intelligent. Leopold was eighteen, and Loeb was nineteen. They were quickly apprehended when Leopold's glasses were discovered near the corpse. Clarence Darrow defended them in court, pleading eloquently against capital punishment. Darrow succeeded, and they were sentenced to life in prison. Loeb was killed in a prison brawl in 1936. Leopold was paroled in 1958; he died in Puerto Rico in 1971.

WRITING THE PLAY

MY twenty-year journey with Leopold and Loeb began in 1977 in the Millburn Public Library in Millburn, New Jersey. I was in high school, shelving books as part of my after-school job. The blood-red binding of a book called *Compulsion* by Meyer Levin caught my eye. I read most of the book waiting in gas lines in my Ford Pinto. Actually, it was my brother's Pinto, solemnly handed down to me when I got my license. That's how things work in New Jersey.

Compulsion is a wonderfully lurid fictionalized account of the Leopold and Loeb story. Barely fictionalized at that. Only legal pressures kept Levin from using the actual names and places. What immediately captured my adolescent fancy was the complex, provocative relationship between Leopold and Loeb. What vexed me were the evasions forced upon Levin. Writing in 1956, Levin had to artfully avoid the true brutality of the murder and any bold pronouncements as to the exact nature of the relationship between the Leopold and Loeb characters. He could only hint at the homosexual aspect of the story.

Above all, the "why" of the story stayed with me. Why did they do it? Why would two young men with every advantage in the world decide to murder an innocent fourteen-year-old boy? What were the demons lurking behind Loeb's flashing good looks? Behind Leopold's saturnine intellect? Those questions have stayed with me—and stimulated my continual work on the play—for the past twenty years.

Five years after my shelving duties in Millburn I was a senior in the theater department at Northwestern University in Evanston, Illinois. On a lark, I decided to take a playwriting class. I had never written a thing before, but thought I would take a stab at it. The object of the year-long class, taught by Linda Jenkins, was to complete a full-length play. Casting my mind around for something to write about, it wasn't long before I came back to Leopold and Loeb. Linda was immediately supportive and suggested I take advantage of the close proximity of Chicago to dive into research.

As the fates would have it, the treasure trove on Leopold and Loeb was a mere fifty yards from the theater building. The Northwestern Library Special Collections is home to the Elmer Gertz Collection. Elmer Gertz was Leopold's parole attorney later in life and had amassed an astounding volume of information on the case. Almost everything. To get access to this material I had to have personal permission from Mr. Gertz. No one but reputed scholars had been allowed to view all the material. I was not, needless to say, a scholar. I was barely even a dramatist.

Nonetheless, I was amazed to learn that Mr. Gertz was willing to meet with me and hear me out. Elmer Gertz is a true legend in Chicago—a legal lion who accepted the mantle of humane jurisprudence from Clarence Darrow and lives by a profound ethical code. My respect for him could not have been, and could not be, higher.

He invited me to his club, and we had lunch. With all the stumbling zealotry of a twenty-one-year-old true believer, I made my case. I told him I wanted to tell the true story. I told him I needed insight into Leopold and Loeb. I told him that only his material could give me the insight I needed. I practically sang arias on the table, my Irish blood exploding in great torrents of words. After my exhausting pitch, he leaned back, smiled, and started talking very quietly about Leopold and Loeb. Then I was talking. Then we were talking together. It remains one of the most exciting moments of my life. From that day to this, Mr. Gertz has been a champion of both myself and the play.

So the gates were unlocked, and the pages spilled forth. I buried myself in Leopold and Loeb. I read an endless stream of intimate letters between Leopold and Loeb and Darrow. I read one of the two existing copies of the full trial transcript. I read dozens of encyclopedic psychiatric reports made at the time of the trial. I held the actual ransom note in my hands. I devoured newspapers from the day, from stories on the case to the comics to the wedding announcements. I hunted down every legal cite and every contemporary reference. I scoured the Chicago Tribune morgue and the Chicago Historical Society for photos. I haunted the areas in Chicago where the events occurred. I watched hours of newsreels, I listened only to music from the period. I read only the books Leopold and Loeb read. My apartment was a chaos of period street maps and phrenology charts and time lines and Nietzsche quotes and ornithology texts and police reports and the whole swirling world of 1924 Chicago.

My friends, quite sensibly, thought I had gone mad.

I was not mad. I was seduced. I was completely captivated by Leopold and Loeb. Their flash and glimmer and panache and smug brilliance had taken hold. To my mind, they were the two most magical human beings who had ever lived.

All that ended on the single most important day in the writing of this play. I was flipping through a very dusty file (from a source who must still remain confidential) when a photo caught my eye. And then another. And another. I was holding the autopsy photographs of Bobby Franks.

Then I wrote the play.

DEVELOPING THE PLAY

THE first version of Never the Sinner was produced at Northwestern in 1983 at the end of my senior year. It was directed by my friend John Swanbeck, who was to prove the first of many invaluable collaborators I would have among directors. On opening night the play ran three hours and had almost 30 characters, including Clarence Darrow's wife, Mrs. Franks, and almost everyone who had ever met Leopold and Loeb. My feeling, which seemed ever so sane at the time, was that the audience would be as profoundly interested in every minute permutation of the story as I was. Also I had done the research, goddamn it, and they were going to know it!

The production was a huge success, although some audience members felt the play was a bit, well, longish.

Not long after that production, I had dinner with my mentor, North-western acting teacher David Downs. Although I was very much a writer by then, I knew that the grounding David had given me in the masterworks of drama had formed the basis of my passion for the form. He is an extraordinary man and a compelling educator. At this dinner I was yammering on enthusiastically about the Important Topics of the play: crime and punishment, the press, the times, homophobia, Darrow's humanism, Nietzsche's philosophy, the end of the Jazz Age, etc. Finally my gush of words abated momentarily as I took a breath, and David just said: "John, it's a love story."

That night I wandered around campus mulling over what

David had said. Then I raced home and called Denis O'Hare, the actor who had played Leopold (and would go on to play Leopold brilliantly in the first major productions in Chicago and London), "Denis," I screeched, "forget everything I ever said. It's a love story!" Denis replied, "I already know that, John." And promptly went back to sleep.

And so it was to become. A very dark, very serpentine love story.

With the tenacious support of Terry McCabe, who directed the first professional Chicago production, I began cutting the play back. Slashing those facets of the story not somehow tied into the beating heart of Leopold and Loeb. I began to use the chorus of three reporters more directly to create the frenzied atmosphere of Chicago at the time. When we opened, the play ran just over two hours and had seven actors. With the committed work of actors like Donna Powers Branson in Chicago and Denis O'Hare and Ben Daniels in London, I tried to shape the spine of the play so that it charted more elegantly the intricate ebbs and flows of the relationship between Leopold and Loeb.

After the West End premiere, I started to find a balance between the characters of Leopold and Loeb. Leopold's journey to something approaching remorse in the play was always more evident to me. The blithe and lethal Richard Loeb, however, remained more enigmatic. After important discussions with my friend Ann Hartdegen, I tried to delve more deeply into Loeb's sad and nihilistic heart. He emerged for me as a more interesting, and strangely poignant, character.

I spent the next ten years working on the play through various productions—cannibalizing the ideas of talented producers, directors, designers, and actors. I wrote 14 other plays in between endless drafts of *Never the Sinner*. To spend this amount of time reshaping a single play is almost unheard of among playwrights. The only defense I can give to this obsessive commitment is that I knew it wasn't right. I knew the elusive characters of Leopold and Loeb remained somehow out of reach. I knew I had not yet captured them to the best of my ability.

The play was finally completed, oddly enough, halfway around the world from where it began. In 1994 the Independent Theatre in Adelaide, Australia, asked to do the play. Because I had previously developed great respect for the director of the company, Rob Croser, I agreed, with one condition: they could mount the play if I could come to Australia and really work on the script with them. Rob and the company were excited by the idea, so off I went to Adelaide, and the work began. Rob and I spent hour after hour twisting the play back and forth. We both agreed that Leopold and Loeb were fading in the second act as Clarence Darrow's titanic influence took over. It was becoming too much Darrow's play.

Sitting on Rob's living room floor, huddled next to an inadequate space heater, I cut much of Darrow's legal maneuvering and wrote a new opening to Act Two as well as two other new scenes for Leopold and Loeb, along with many revisions. We tossed new material to the actors on an almost daily basis; they rose to the challenge with enthusiasm and superhuman patience.

The script I developed in Australia—with some terrific final cuts made with the vastly talented director Ethan McSweeny for the New York production—is the play you are holding.

LEAVING THE PLAY

AFTER twenty years, my journey with Leopold and Loeb is over,

I have created a story that I think is honest. I hope I have been true to the absolute cruelty of the characters and the senseless savagery of their crime, while still presenting the very human passions that compelled them.

In the end, I feel great pity for Leopold and Loeb. They longed to create a private world of fevered intellect and romantic passion. They ended up creating nothing but degradation and despair and death.

To say that Leopold and Loeb were "monsters" is too easy. To say that they were "evil" is too facile. I find Darrow's tact more relevant. Leopold and Loeb were human beings. Just like the rest of us. They were tormented. They were brutal. They lacked any true moral, ethical compass. They could not find their way in our sunlit world, so they embraced the darkness. In that darkness they only had each other.

The real provocation of Leopold and Loeb is that we all could, given some unkind twists of fate and character, be them. We have all loved someone too much. We have all had our hearts broken. We have all wanted to prove our everlasting devotion. We have all looked quietly at our loved one across the room and thought to ourselves, "I'd die for you ... I'd kill for you ..."

This is, I suppose, a cautionary tale.

—JOHN LOGAN
June, 1998

"Now once more the belt is tight and we summon up the proper expression of horror as we look back at our wasted youth. Sometimes, though, there is a ghostly rumble among the drums, an asthmatic whisper in the trombones that swing us back to the early years of the twenties when we drank wood alcohol and in every day and in every way grew better and better, there was the first of the abortive shortening of the skirts, and girls all looked alike in sweater dresses, and it seemed only a matter of time before the older people would step aside and let the world be run by those who saw things as they really were—and it all seems rosy and romantic to us who were young then, because we will never feel quite so intensely about our surroundings any more.

—F. SCOTT FITZGERALD, "Echoes of the Jazz Age"

ACT 1

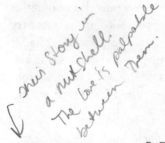

their story in a nutshell.
The love is palpable
between them.

SCENE 1

(Lights up to reveal LEOPOLD giving a lecture on ornithology. He wipes his glasses nervously as he speaks. He speaks directly to the audience. LOEB is seated behind him. LEOPOLD is made increasingly nervous by LOEB's presence.)

Luke knows this

LEOPOLD

The Prairie Falcon makes little fuss over the capture of small game—that is to say, over the capture of game smaller than itself. It simply materializes out of the blue and picks up a gopher or smaller bird the way you or I would pluck a flower. Its approach, no doubt, has been well-calculated. The falcon, launched from a height of half a mile to a mile, controls his swoop through a slight opening of the wings; this is to check the cadence and intent of the victim; the final plunge, therefore, has the speed and accuracy of . . . fate. In the case of game larger than itself, the quarry is knocked headlong by a crashing blow to the skull. When the falcon's nest has been disturbed, the huge bird will swoop high into the air and turn . . . for the . . . um . . . for a . . . a vicious attack.

(LOEB *laughs quietly.* LEOPOLD *pauses for a moment.*)

It is a strong, bold, fearless fighter. But it is wary, shy and secretive when it is threatened or has been subject to molestation. Like most other hawks it likes to sit on dead trees and other conspicuous perches that will give it a wide outlook over the domain it considers to be its own.

Now, as this is our first trip into the field I will remind you of a few of our prime birding rules. First, we must be as quiet as possible so as not to frighten off our prey. Second, we must try to blend into the environment as naturally as possible. Finally, we must watch our step: there are culverts and channels in the marshes which could cause serious injury if you were to fall into them. All right then, head out to the cars and I will meet you in a moment.

(LEOPOLD *watches as they go. He finally spins to confront* LOEB. LOEB *smiles and snaps his fingers as if to say,* "Nothing to it. It'll be a piece of cake.")

(*Lights cross fade to...*)

SCENE 2
(*The courtroom.*)

REPORTER 1
From the vantage point of the crowded press box, we saw them enter. Leopold, dark and brooding—shifting impatiently as his handcuffs were removed. Loeb, bright and airy—flashing his killer smile and cutting his way through the crowd like an expert tango dancer.

REPORTER 3
July 21st, 1924. Leopold and Loeb Trial Begins Today!

REPORTER 2
The temperature in the packed courtroom soared to a stifling ninety-seven degrees, but Leopold and Loeb appeared oblivious to the heat and looked disarmingly spry in their perfectly tai-lored suits and Valentino-slick hair.

REPORTER 3

Were it not for the innumerable sheriff's deputies gathered around them, one could well imagine them being here to do research for a college paper on the workings of the Hall of Justice.

REPORTER 1

Clarence Darrow, Attorney for the Defense, entered the courtroom loaded down with weathered law books—

REPORTER 2

His battered old briefcase bearing the scars of his numerous courtroom brawls—

REPORTER 3

While State's Attorney Robert Crowe stalked in—a slick symphony of sinewy ambition.

REPORTER 2

At last all is silent, and the Trial of the Century is suddenly upon us...

BAILIFF   *Rep.¹*

The People of the State of Illinois versus Nathan Leopold, Jr. and Richard Loeb for the crime of murder, before the Honorable Judge John R. Caverly in the Criminal Court of Cook County, at the July term, A.D. 1924. All rise.

(*Lights cross fade to...*)

SCENE 3

(LOEB *sits.* LEOPOLD *stands.*)

LOEB

Do *Ubermensch* dance?

(*Beat.*)

LEOPOLD

I beg your pardon?

LOEB

Do *Ubermensch* dance?

(LOEB *laughs.*)

LEOPOLD

Are you going to take this seriously or not?

LOEB

Oh, yes, please go on.

(*Beat.* LEOPOLD *continues:*)

Luke needs to read Nietzsche about this.

LEOPOLD

The *Ubermensch*—the *Superman*—as Nietzsche envisioned him is aloof to the petty concerns of mankind. He must recognize his superiority and exercise his free will without regard for the feelings of the rest of humanity. He has earned the right to this supreme indifference through his advanced status. The superman is exempt from the laws that bind the common run of humanity. He lives in a realm that transcends the body politic.

LOEB

Above.

LEOPOLD

Yes. Above humanity. The superman's mind and soul are filled with noble thoughts and profound philosophy that would blind normal people. He feels no obligation to be limited by the social, religious, and moral conventions of his contemporaries. Their paltry laws and ethics pale to insignificance before him.

LOEB

Hm.

LEOPOLD

So you begin to understand the awesome responsibility of the *Ubermensch.*

LOEB

To live up to his exalted potential, yes. To be remembered.

LEOPOLD

Yes.

LOEB

To stun the world.

(*Beat.*)

LEOPOLD

Yes.

LOEB

All right, professor, lesson's over. My turn to play teacher.

(LOEB *stands and puts out his hands to* LEOPOLD)

LEOPOLD

Oh no...

LOEB

Come on now, you promised...

(LOEB *takes* LEOPOLD *and waltzes with him.* LEOPOLD *is unsteady. As they dance...*)

LOEB

And... One-two-three-one-two-three-one-two-three—are you counting, Babe?

LEOPOLD

I'm counting in my head.

LOEB

Apparently your feet can't hear.

LEOPOLD

How about letting me lead?

LOEB

You can't even follow yet.

LEOPOLD

But I won't have to follow.

LOEB

Ah—but you do now!

(LOEB *laughs as he spins* LEOPOLD *around the stage.*)

(*Lights cross fade to…*)

SCENE 4

(CROWE *in the courtroom.*)

CROWE

Your Honor, I ask you to look at these two young men. I ask you to look at their expensively cut suits and their slicked-back hair and the smirks on their faces. I ask you to consider the way they have deported themselves in this court, their every action a mockery of these proceedings. Consider how they must have smiled as they methodically cruised the streets of Kenwood in search of their victim. Consider their smiles as they seduced little Bobby Franks into their car. As they pulled shut the door and mercilessly beat him to death. As they stripped his body. As they pushed him into that sewer.

Consider their smiles…

(*Lights cross fade to…*)

(GERMAINE RHEINHARDT *stands alone.* LOEB *bursts in on her.*)

LOEB

Germaine!

GERMAINE

Dick, you're on time!

(*He spins her around in the air.*)

LOEB

Ah, my little gold-digger.

GERMAINE (*Laughing*)

Dick, you're nuts!

LOEB

Only nuts for you, sweetest!

(*He kisses her quickly.* LEOPOLD *appears behind* LOEB.)

GERMAINE

Oh . . . hello.

LOEB

Germaine, this is my best chum in all the world, Nathan Leopold.

GERMAINE (*Putting out her hand*)

Gosh, nice to finally meet you.

LEOPOLD (*Ignoring her hand*)

Gosh, you too.

LOEB (*To* GERMAINE)

Now, don't let those big bug eyes scare you off. Babe's really a great guy.

GERMAINE

Babe?

LOEB

That's what I call him.

LEOPOLD

Sort of nickname, Miss Rheinhardt.

LOEB

Miss Rheinhardt my ass—call her Germaine.

LEOPOLD

As you like.

LOEB (*To* GERMAINE)

And you've got to call him Babe. He's my best—you two have got
to be the best of pals, okay?

GERMAINE

Dick, could I... um... talk to you for a second?

LOEB

Sure, what's up?

LEOPOLD

It seems the young lady would like to speak with you alone.

LOEB

Alone?

GERMAINE

Yes. Well...

LEOPOLD

Perhaps I should go...

LOEB

Don't be silly. What's up, Germaine?

(*Beat.*)

GERMAINE

Well, Dick, I thought we were going to have... you know, a...

LEOPOLD

A special evening alone?

GERMAINE

Well, yes.

LEOPOLD

How quaint.

LOEB (*To* LEOPOLD)

Stop it.

(*To* GERMAINE)

Oh, Babe can come along, can't he? He is really the greatest guy, really and truly. Would I lie to you? How could I lie to those big brown eyes? Now could we please get going? The night is young and we're getting older by the moment. I thought we could go by the Drake and—

GERMAINE

But Dick, we promised Max and Gladys—

LOEB

Oh fuck Max and Gladys—

GERMAINE

Dick!

LOEB

I mean they're no fun anyway, are they?

(*To* LEOPOLD)

Babe, you should really meet them though—troglodytes both.

(*They laugh.*)

GERMAINE

It's just that we promised—

LOEB

Well I promised Babe too.

(*Beat.*)

GERMAINE

Dick, you said—

LOEB

And I promised Babe first.

(*Beat.*)

GERMAINE

Okay. Why don't you two go on then.

LOEB

You sure it's okay?

GERMAINE

Sure.

LOEB

Truly?

GERMAINE

Sure.

LOEB

All right then, honey. Call me tomorrow early in the
a.m.—well not too early ...

(*He kisses her quickly and begins to leave.*)

Have fun with Max and Gladys.

LEOPOLD (*Taking her hand
quickly and shaking it*)

A pleasure to have met you, Miss Rheinhardt.

(LEOPOLD *exits quickly after* LOEB. *Lights cross fade to*
Crowe.)

CROWE

Your Honor, I ask you to tear those superior smirks from their
faces. I ask you to send a message across the land that we will not
allow this capricious disregard for the morality and laws of our
country. I ask you for the extreme penalty. For death.

(*Lights cross fade to...*)

SCENE 5

(LEOPOLD *sits.* LOEB *enters quickly.*)

LOEB

Hiya, sport, how ya doing?

LEOPOLD

Just grand.

LOEB

Okay, Nietzsche, here's the plan. You're gonna love this! We go
to Lincoln Park and wait until some poor Joe is passing and
then—pow!—we walk up like we got gats in our coats and I say,
"Now listen, Mister, you give us your wallet or my ugly friend

here," that's you, "will drill ya." And you look all tough and quiet, okay? You can be quiet for ten minutes, Babe?

LEOPOLD

I—

LOEB

Then you snarl at him or something and I say, "Lookee here, Bub, my pal's got an itchy trigger finger so give over with the loot but pronto." So he gives us his wallet and then maybe we rough him up a bit, just to make it all look real.

LEOPOLD

Sounds pretty real to me.

LOEB

Yeah, I got handkerchiefs in the car so we can hide our faces.

LEOPOLD

Handkerchiefs?

LOEB

Sure, don't you ever read anything but Shakespeare, Babe? Ya gotta have handkerchiefs so he can't finger us to the cops!

LEOPOLD

Wait a minute—

LOEB

Oh, come on, it'll be a hoot. Some poor nobody gets the shit scared out of him and we get maybe fifty bucks or so. We'll look for somebody with real slick threads. Patent leathers too—

LEOPOLD

Dick, I'm not really sure about this.

(LOEB *stops.*)

LOEB

What do you mean?

LEOPOLD

Can't we do something else?

LOEB

Bridge again? Or maybe you wanna go bird watching? Grow up, Babe!

LEOPOLD

What if the police—

LOEB

The cops are a bunch of flat-foot louts and you know it. It'll be a piece of cake.

LEOPOLD

I'm not sure, Dick—

LOEB

Afraid, Babe?

LEOPOLD

No. But it's pointless.

LOEB

Wrong, it's the only thing that has a point.

(*Beat.*)

You're pathetic. Some Superman.

(*He turns to go.*)

LEOPOLD

Wait, Dick—

(LOEB *turns. Suddenly fierce:*)

LOEB

If you can't take it, then forget it! I'll find someone who's good for a few laughs. You're useless. I could just kill you like that —

(*Snaps his fingers.*)

You're nothing!

LEOPOLD

No, don't go! I'm sorry. I just don't know about this...

LOEB

What's to know?

(*He moves close to* LEOPOLD.)

You and me, boy-o. What couldn't we do if we wanted?

LEOPOLD

I'm just not interested in robbery.

LOEB

What are you interested in then?

(*Beat.*)

You do this and you'll find it very fulfilling, I promise you.

(*He touches* LEOPOLD.)

Just think of the way that poor sucker'll look at us! Blinded by us. We could make him do anything. He will be in our power. Our *absolute power*, Babe.

(*Beat.*)

Philosophies are meant to be lived. Think about it, kiddo.

(*Lights cross fade to...*)

SCENE 6

(LEOPOLD *and* LOEB *at a table.* CROWE *stands.*)

CROWE

Nathan, would you describe for me please the condition of the body when you placed it in the culvert?

LEOPOLD

Condition?

CROWE

Yes.

LOEB

Deceased.

(*He and* LEOPOLD *laugh.*)

CROWE

Physically, please. The condition of the body.

LEOPOLD

There was a small, sharp wound three-quarters of an inch in length on the right side of the cranium near the hair-line. A second wound could be located on the left side about an inch above the supraorbital nerve.

CROWE

And the back of the head, did you notice?

LEOPOLD

There were two sharp wounds in the parietal region, both running longitudinally for about half an inch. The deepest of these, which I assume was from the first blow, was located on the left side of the cranium equally between the sagittal and lambdoidal sutures. There was also some swelling and bruises.

CROWE

On the back of the head?

LEOPOLD

Yes.

CROWE

I see.

(*Beat.*)

CROWE

These wounds were caused by the chisel?

LEOPOLD

They were.

CROWE

Go on. What was the condition of the face?

LEOPOLD

The pigmentation of the face was discolored to a...

(*He turns to* LOEB.)

What would you say?

LOEB

A pleasant copper color.

LEOPOLD

Yes, discolored to a pleasant copper color as far down as the mouth. I assume this is from the irritant we poured on it to disfigure the face.

CROWE

The irritant?

LEOPOLD

Yes.

CROWE

And what was the irritant, Nathan?

(*Beat.*)

LEOPOLD

Hydrochloric acid.

CROWE

Yes, hydrochloric acid, thank you.

(*Beat.*)

Let me read you a section from the coroner's report. "On examining the torso I discovered several small scratches extending from the right shoulder blade to the buttocks and a few superficial scratches on the forehead. The rectum was dilated and could easily admit one middle finger..."

(LOEB *giggles softly and whispers to* LEOPOLD.)

"On opening the body I found a dark discoloration extending down the windpipe into the right lung as far as the diaphragm, caused by absorption of fumes and suffocation. It is our expert view that Robert Franks came to his death from an injury to the head, complicated by suffocation."

(*Beat.* CROWE *looks at them.*)

LEOPOLD

That sounds about right.

(*Beat.* CROWE *starts to go. Stops.*)

CROWE

Was there a lot of blood?

LOEB

Not an inordinate amount.

(*Lights cross fade to...*)

SCENE 7

(LEOPOLD *stands*. LOEB *paces*.)

LOEB

Who? Who? Who?

LEOPOLD

Someone defenseless.

LOEB

Someone *weak*.

LEOPOLD

How about one of our fathers? It could be an act of consanguineous revenge?

LOEB

I am truly ashamed for having allied myself with such an ignorant gang. Now think: if your father were to be suddenly kidnapped you would be thrust, so to speak, into the public eye. You would be an immediate suspect: *Young Millionaire Kidnaps Own Father: Could It Be Consanguineous Revenge?*

LEOPOLD

I bow to your superior wisdom.

LOEB

As ever. What we need is some weak little fellow whose father has bags and bags of cash just sitting around the palatial estate.

LEOPOLD

Some young fellow?

LOEB

Yes.

LEOPOLD

How about your brother?

LOEB

Hmm... No, no, no—too many eager policeman hunting about the house; they might just find that tiny incriminating clue that had escaped us.

LEOPOLD

Unlikely.

LOEB

Besides, it might upset Mom. Someone else.

(*They pace and think.* LEOPOLD *stops.*)

LEOPOLD

I've got it! I know who it is we're going to get.

LOEB

All right, boy wonder, who?

LEOPOLD (*Proudly*)

Hamlin Buchman!

LOEB

Who?

LEOPOLD

Hamlin Buchman! You remember, that bastard who started all those rumors about us—

LOEB

In Michigan—

LEOPOLD

It would be so fitting to censure that salacious little prick. And think of the poetic justice!

LOEB

Poetic justice will not get us any ransom. My dear fellow, if we were to remove this rather obvious enemy, we would be under immediate suspicion. Besides that, he's obese—

LEOPOLD

Well, that's true.

LOEB

If you want to deal with five hundred pounds of Hamlin Buchman be my guest...

LEOPOLD

No.

LOEB

I'm not going to.

> (*Pause as* LOEB *paces back and forth with nervous energy. He stops and spins to* LEOPOLD.)

LOEB

I've got it! Richard Rubel!

LEOPOLD

Dick Rubel...?

LOEB (*With typical histrionics*)

Of course! Think of it, we'd be sure to be asked to be pallbearers, or at least I would—sorry, Babe—you'd have to sit this one out and watch from the sidelines, all very serious of course.

Imagine: I'd arrive at his house, dignified and gray in my funereal best—a simple cut, single breasted, you know the type.

I'd walk up to Mrs. Rubel and extend my hand with a slight tremor brought on by the profundity of the moment. "Mrs. Rubel," I'd say, "I just wanted you to know"—a slight tear here maybe—"you have no idea how important Dick was to me." She'd shake my hand, properly moved by my sentiment, and depart with solemn grace to the back of the house. The house! The whole house is wreathed in black, shrouds and wreaths everywhere, in raven silk and crinoline.

Finally, we'd be led into the sitting room or somewhere where they'd be hiding the coffin, all shining and black ebony or something suitably glimmering. All the pallbearers shake hands, dripping pathos and tragedy. Perhaps I could work in a faint, ya think? Well, anyway, we'd take up the casket—ah, a bit heavier than we had first imagined. Do we drop it? No, that's too much. Finally we hoist up ol' Dick onto our shoulders and proceed—with stately cadence—to maneuver Dick through the tight hallways and then we burst into the bright sunlight. The passers-by and the newsmen, of course they'd be flashing pictures, they would all sympathetically doff their hats—definitely tears here—and we would march past them with.... too much... humanity... to bear.

(*He spins on* LEOPOLD.)

And no one but you and I to know who done it!!

(*Beat.*)

LEOPOLD
Dick Rubel is almost as fat as Hamlin Buchman.

LOEB
Boy, you simply won't give into a poetic moment, will ya?

(*They laugh.*)

LOEB
All right then, who's it going to be?

LEOPOLD

Johnny Levinson?

LOEB

Maybe...

LEOPOLD

Bobby Franks?

LOEB

Could be...

LEOPOLD

Irving Hartman?

LOEB

Better and better...

LEOPOLD

Army Deutsch?

LOEB

So many nasty little boys—our problem is merely one of *selection*. Simple, simple. Who...? Who...? Who...?

LEOPOLD (*Suddenly*)
Why don't we leave it to the gods?

(*Beat.*)

LOEB

Exactly how do you mean that?

LEOPOLD

I mean leave it to fate! Why don't we just cruise the Harvard School area and take whomever best fits us—

LOEB

Just pick the first flower that smells right...?

LEOPOLD

Exactly! *Amor fati!*

LOEB

We could leave the name on the ransom note blank and—

LEOPOLD

And fill it in when we have our guest!

LOEB

Oh, my dear boy, forget my comments as to your poetic sensi-
bilities—or lack therein—this plan is the stuff of genius!

(LEOPOLD *smiles and moves closer to* LOEB. LOEB *glances
at his watch and moves away.*)

LOEB

Christ! I've got to go... I hope Mom's not up. Where could I have
been tonight?

LEOPOLD

Germaine's?

LOEB

No, I said I was with Germaine last night.

LEOPOLD

The library?

LOEB

Yes! Scholarly, she'll love that.
    We leave it to fate then.

(*He takes* LEOPOLD's *hand and shakes it.*)

Our pact. We leave it to the gods.

(LOEB *heads out quickly—he is almost gone when he suddenly stops and then races back to* LEOPOLD. *He grabs* LEOPOLD's *face and kisses him passionately, almost with violence, and then races off.*)

(*Lights cross fade to...*)

SCENE 8

(LEOPOLD *and* DR. BOWMAN *sit together.* LOEB *and* DR. HULBERT *sit together. They are in separate rooms at the jail.*)

LEOPOLD

Making up my mind to commit murder was practically like deciding whether or not I'd eat pie for dinner. The question was: would it give me pleasure?

HULBERT (*To* LOEB)

Dick, you have got to have some reaction to what you did. Something ... anger, pride, puzzlement, fear?

LOEB (*Nicely*)

Nope.

LEOPOLD

I was trying to break down any feelings of affection that I had for my family. I have tried to kill all such affection for years.

HULBERT

On the afternoon of the murder, you stopped at a hot dog stand for a snack, right?

LOEB

Yeah, I had a hot dog with mustard and relish too, I think. Babe didn't have anything.

HULBERT

And Bobby Franks' body was wrapped in a rug on the back seat all the while?

LOEB

Yes.

HULBERT

Dick, why do you think you stopped to eat?

LOEB

I was hungry.

LEOPOLD

My mother's death is one of the things which has most profoundly affected my philosophy of life. It seems to me that if God took away such a wonderful and exceptional person as my mother, then that God is a callous and a selfish God, and I do not care to worship him.

LOEB

Oh yes, I also had a glass of milk.

LEOPOLD

After my mother's death, I realized that if I could kid myself into the belief that there was a life hereafter, I could be happy... But I felt I must be intellectually honest.

LOEB

I've always had this fantasy about being the head of a criminal gang.

HULBERT

What was the gang like?

LOEB

It was a huge serpentine organization, and I sat at the center and controlled all the permutations. Just like Al Capone; at the center of a tenacious web of crime...

LEOPOLD

Dick fantasizes a lot. When he begins to develop a fantasy, he starts off with the expression...

LOEB

And you know, Teddy.

LEOPOLD

This is a continuance into his present life of a practice that was his as an infant. He used to take a teddy bear to bed with him; and then he would say, "And you know, Teddy," and all his fantasies would pour forth.

LOEB

And I would be in charge of all the operations. Ruthless, with a scar, you know.

(*He laughs.*)

HULBERT

What sort of crime was the gang involved in?

LOEB

Oh, forgery, smuggling, robbery—

HULBERT

Kidnapping?

(*Beat.*)

LOEB (*Smiles*)

Perhaps.

BOWMAN

Babe, you have an astounding knowledge of philology. It says here that you can speak fourteen—

LEOPOLD

Fifteen.

BOWMAN

Different languages. Fifteen?

LEOPOLD (*Smiles*)

Yes, I'm taking a correspondence course in Sanskrit.

HULBERT

How did the other criminals in the gang look at you?

LOEB

They worshipped me.

BOWMAN

Did you ever meet any of Dick's girlfriends?

LEOPOLD

Yes, one.

BOWMAN

And...?

LEOPOLD

I didn't much care for her.

BOWMAN

Why's that?

(*Beat.*)

LEOPOLD

She had an unfortunate penchant for saying, "Gosh."

HULBERT

Did you have lots of girlfriends?

LOEB

Enough.

HULBERT

Nathan have a lot too?

LOEB (*Smiles*)

Nathan is rather restrained.

HULBERT

I see. Did he have a lot of friends?

LOEB

Not really.

HULBERT

Are you his best friend?

LOEB

I suppose I am.

HULBERT

Are you his only friend?

(LOEB *does not respond.*)

BOWMAN

Would you say that you make friends easily?

LEOPOLD

I wouldn't say so, no.

BOWMAN

Did you have many puppy love affairs when you were growing up?

LEOPOLD

"Puppy love affairs"? No.

HULBERT

According to your baby book, you laughed at four weeks and learned your first words from your German governess at four months: "Nein, nein, Mama." You walked at five months and said your first prayer at age three—

LOEB

"Ich bin klein, mein herz ist rein." I am small, my heart is pure.

BOWMAN

It's a pretty standard psychological exercise. You just tell me the first word that pops into your head. For example, I might say "hot" and you might say—

LEOPOLD

Cold. Got it.

BOWMAN

All right. Day.

LEOPOLD

Night.

BOWMAN

Father.

LEOPOLD

Bank.

BOWMAN

Sky.

LEOPOLD

Bird.

BOWMAN

Doctor.

LEOPOLD

Tedious.

(*Beat.*)

BOWMAN

Drink.

LEOPOLD

Flask.

BOWMAN

Al Jolson.

LEOPOLD

Mammy.

BOWMAN

Blood.

LEOPOLD

Sticky.

BOWMAN

Snow.

LEOPOLD

Fall.

BOWMAN

Richard Loeb.

(LEOPOLD *pauses. He shakes his finger at* BOWMAN *and laughs.*)

HULBERT

Day.

LOEB

Time.

HULBERT

Night.

LOEB

Dance.

HULBERT

Girl.

LOEB

Silky.

HULBERT

Hair.

LOEB

Valentino.

HULBERT

Boy.

LOEB

Baseball

HULBERT

Cat.

LOEB

Spine.

HULBERT

Father.

LOEB

Mother.

HULBERT

Murder.

(*Beat.*)

LOEB

Newspaper.

BOWMAN

Did Dick have lots of friends?

LEOPOLD

Yes, tons.

BOWMAN

That bother you?

(*Beat.*)

LEOPOLD

"From hence your memory death cannot take, Though in me each part will be forgotten."

BOWMAN

That's nice.

LEOPOLD

It's Shakespeare.

BOWMAN

I know. Sonnet 81.

(LEOPOLD *raises an eyebrow in surprise.*)

LOEB

Well, Babe used to tell me about this one fantasy he would have. He used to call it "The King and the Slave." He was sometimes the King and sometimes the Slave. But mostly he was the Slave...

LEOPOLD

In some way or other I usually saved the life of the King. The King, who was always very strong and exceptionally beautiful, was grateful and wanted to give me my freedom, but I always refused.

There were often King's banquets where each King brought his body slave to serve as his champion in mortal combat. I would fight for hours for the honor of my King. I always won... We were chained as slaves, but I was chained with only a tiny gold band I could easily have broken...

(*Lights cross fade to...*)

SCENE 9

(*The courtroom.* DR. WHITE, *a psychologist, is on the stand.* CROWE *is casually cross-examining.*)

WHITE

Of course the medical profession demands such psychological classifications. But it is hardly for one, or more than one, of my profession to make any pronouncements as to the psychological stability of patients studied under the most artificial of circumstances. For example, one might cite the analysis of the sexual pact initiated by Leopold and Loeb which was set up in a paralegal format and...

(*The court starts into action.* CROWE *jerks to attention.* DARROW *quickly confers with* LEOPOLD *and* LOEB, *who appear horrified. The reporters scribble notes madly and crane forward. Pause.*)

CROWE

I beg your pardon, Dr. White. Are you referring to a *homosexual* pact made between Leopold and Loeb?

WHITE

Yes.

(*Pause. There is absolute silence in the courtroom.*)

CROWE (*Quietly*)

When was this pact created?

WHITE

Around the middle of November, 1923.

CROWE

Well, Dr. White, what was the substance of this contract?

WHITE

This compact, as told to me by both of the boys, consisted of an agreement that Leopold would be able to... Do you want me to be specific?

CROWE

Absolutely.

WHITE

Well, in essence, their agreement was an even exchange of sexual activity for criminal activity. Leopold would take part in crimes primarily to accommodate Loeb and Loeb would take part in sexual acts primarily to accommodate Leopold. Leopold had the days of sexual interaction marked on a special calendar, and on these certain days Leopold, who has had for many years a great deal of fantasy life surrounding sexual activity, usually with Loeb himself, was to have the opportunity of exploring certain areas that he found to be of...

(As WHITE *fades into silence and darkness,* LEOPOLD *and* LOEB *move downstage. They both sit casually-yet it is one of those "certain days," and both are acutely aware of this.*)

(Pause.)

LOEB

Sure do envy your trip to Europe, Babe.

LEOPOLD

I'm looking forward to it. I should learn a lot.

LOEB

What are you looking forward to most?

LEOPOLD

Oh... Berlin, I suppose. And Athens, Paris, everything really.

(Beat.)

I wish you were coming too.

LOEB

Oh, you'll have a fine time without me. Besides, if I were with you, who would you have to write to?

LEOPOLD

Well, that's true. But I can imagine my anticipation now on the boat on the way home.

(Beat.)

Anticipation can be very rewarding.
  Will you meet me at the dock?

LOEB

Sure. Sure.

(LOEB *shifts uneasily.*)

LEOPOLD

You're nervous.

LOEB

Nonsense.

LEOPOLD

You shouldn't be nervous.

LOEB

I'm not.

LEOPOLD

Okay.

    (*Pause.*)

What's the... uh... date, today?

    (LOEB *doesn't respond.*)

The 16th?

LOEB

I know the date.

LEOPOLD

Well then?

The 16th is one of the days we contracted to—

LOEB (*Very sharply*)
Look, I know that! Just let it rest!

    (*Beat.*)

Christ...

    (*Beat.*)

Sorry, I didn't mean to yell.

LEOPOLD

No—

LOEB

I really—

LEOPOLD

No, it's all right, I understand. But you don't.

LOEB

Don't what?

LEOPOLD

Don't understand.

LOEB

Don't understand what, Babe?

LEOPOLD

Forget it, Dick.

LOEB

No what?

LEOPOLD (*With difficulty,*
not looking at LOEB)

You don't understand how I feel. What it feels like.

(*Pause.*)

LOEB

I can't say anything. There is nothing for me to say, is there? Is there?

(LEOPOLD *looks at him.*)

Is there, Babe?

(LEOPOLD *gently touches* LOEB's *face. He then turns and walks upstage into the darkness.* LOEB *eventually follows.*)

(*Lights up slightly on* WHITE *as he continues his testimony:*)

WHITE

... Leopold says he gets a thrill out of anticipating it, Loeb would often pretend to be drunk, and then Leopold would undress him, and they would be furiously passionate at times... Even in jail, a look at Loeb's body or a touch of his shoulder thrills Leopold, so he says, immeasurably.

(*Lights cross fade to...*)

SCENE 10

REPORTER 1

Body of Boy Found in Swamp!

REPORTER 3   *Jump ↑ on chair*

Kidnapped Rich Boy Found Dead!

REPORTER 2

Bobby Franks Found Dead in Marshes!

REPORTER 1

Police Remove Body from Culvert. Hunt for Clues Begins!

REPORTER 2

What happened? Why? Why? These questions flood through the minds of the citizens of Chicago. And mothers across the city hold their babes a little more closely while the mad killer of little Bobby Franks continues to haunt Chicago.

Move DR

REPORTER 1

The icy finger of suspicion continues to cruise over Chicago, alighting for a moment on this school-teacher, on that postman.

REPORTER 3

May 24th, Bobby Franks Died Fighting!

REPORTER 2

May 25th, State's Attorney Robert Crowe Promises Quick Justice and a Hanging!

REPORTER 1

"I'll Have the Killer Swinging by Christmas!" says "Fighting" Bob Crowe.

REPORTER 3

May 26th, All City Hunts for Killers! Police Call Crime the Strangest and Most Baffling In Chicago History!

REPORTER 1

May 27th, Bobby Franks Buried Today...

(The Reporters stand as if outside the Franks' house and watch the coffin being carried out. LOEB enters and stands with the reporters.)

REPORTER 2

After a brief service at his home today, little Bobby Franks was laid to rest under the quiet arbors of Rosehill cemetery. The crowd was silent and pensive as they watched the solemn corps of Bobby Franks' little school chums carry the tiny coffin from the Franks' home to the waiting hearse. A tiny hearse for a tiny coffin for a tiny body. In the grim faces of the assembled crowd one thought could clearly be seen: who could do such a thing?

(Pause as they watch the hearse drive away.)

LOEB *(Sighs)*

Poor Bobby, I can just see him playing tennis now...

(He begins to move away.)

REPORTER 2

Excuse me, did you actually know Bobby Franks?

LOEB

Sure did. He's my cousin. Or he was my cousin, I guess.

(*The reporters eagerly gather around* LOEB.)

REPORTER 1

What's your name, kid?

LOEB

Richard Loeb. L-O-E-B. I live about four houses down. Ya see that house with the big red gates? Oh, I just feel awful about poor Bobby ... he was so young ...

REPORTER 3

How did you feel when you found out your cousin had been murdered?

LOEB

Gosh, I guess I felt scared. I mean, is no one safe anymore?

REPORTER 2

And how did you feel watching his funeral today?

LOEB

Well, actually all those gray-faced little boys made me nervous.

(*Beat.*)

REPORTER 2

Listen, tell us something about Bobby.

LOEB

Well, he was always a good little tennis player. We used to play at our courts. He always kept his eye on the ball, followed through on his backhand, he was very limber, but ya know how kids are at that age.

REPORTER 2

No, I mean personally what was he like?

LOEB

Oh, I didn't know him very well, really. But he could be pretty annoying at times. You know, arrogant.

REPORTER 2

Really?

LOEB

Yeah, as a matter of fact, if I were going to find someone to kidnap and murder, it would be a cocky little bastard like Bobby Franks.

(*The reporters are stunned.* LOEB *smiles and moves on with:*)

Remember, that's L-O-E-B.

(LOEB *goes.*)

REPORTER 2

May 28th, Al Capone Declares: Organized Crime Not Responsible for Franks Murder.

REPORTER 1

"We Don't Kill Babies," Snarls Scarface Al.

REPORTER 3

Chicago Tribune Offers $5,000 For Any Exclusive Information...

REPORTER 2

Chicago Herald and Examiner Offers *$10,000* For Any New Clues...

REPORTER 3

Police Raid Opium Den for Franks Killer: "Must Be the Work of a Drug-Addicted Mind," Cries Police Commissioner Downs.

REPORTER 1

Police Out In Force, Scouring Crime Scene for Clues.

(*Lights cross fade to...*)

SCENE 11

(LEOPOLD *sits.* LOEB *enters.*)

LEOPOLD

Dick! Did Sam let you up—

LOEB (*Tense*)

No, I just came up—

(*He continues carefully, darkly.*)

Where are your glasses, Babe?

LEOPOLD

What?

LOEB

Your glasses, where are they?

LEOPOLD (*Feeling for glasses*)

They must be in another jacket...

LOEB

No, they're not.

LEOPOLD

No?

LOEB

No.

LEOPOLD

Where are they?

LOEB (*Hisses*)

The police have them.

LEOPOLD

What?

(LOEB *throws a newspaper at* LEOPOLD. LEOPOLD *reads furiously.*)

REPORTER 1

Glasses Found by Body!

LEOPOLD

Oh God.

REPORTER 2

Police theorize that if the owner of the glasses found by Bobby Franks' body can be located, the killer must be close by!

LEOPOLD (*Stepping toward* LOEB)

No. I'm sure my glasses are in my other coat—I couldn't have dropped them—Dick, I didn't, I swear—

(LOEB *spins on him ferociously.*)

LOEB

How could you have done this? You dropped your fucking glasses!

(LOEB *stalks the room.*)

LOEB

Right by the body! Great! Why didn't you just leave a note with your address?

REPORTER 1

Chicago Daily News, May 29th: Murder Glasses a Rare Prescription. Arrests Promised!

REPORTER 3

Optometrists Work Day and Night to Trace Franks Murder Glasses.

REPORTER 2

Cop House Buzz: Crowe Sniffs Out Owner of Murder Specs...

(LEOPOLD *and* LOEB *go to separate chairs.* CROWE *walks between them. They are being interrogated separately.*)

CROWE

... on the 21st?

LOEB

We had lunch at the Marshall Fields Grill, and then Babe wanted to go bird-watching in Lincoln Park. So I thought, what the hell, there's all sorts of birds, if ya catch my meaning...

LEOPOLD

Dick brought along a flask of gin and a flask of scotch, so I'm afraid we didn't get a great deal of bird-watching done that afternoon!

REPORTER 2

May 30th, Suspect Brought in on Franks Case! Link to Glasses Found by the Body.

CROWE

Scotch and gin, are you quite sure about that?

LEOPOLD

Quite sure. Yes.

LOEB

Well, Babe didn't want to go home with liquor on his breath so we had dinner at the Coconut Grove on 53rd and Ellis. You know it?

CROWE

No.

LOEB

It's very nice.

CROWE

I'm sure.

LEOPOLD

So after dinner we cruised along 63rd, looking for girls.

CROWE

Looking for girls?

LEOPOLD

For girls.

REPORTER 3

Two Suspects Questioned In Franks Murder!

LOEB

So we picked up these two hotsies named Mae and Edna on 63rd but they wouldn't put out—you know how that is.

CROWE

What did they look like?

LOEB

Edna was this real red-head dish, and Mae was more ... pulchritudinous. Dark hair. Some sort of mole on her cheek. Or maybe it was a scar.

LEOPOLD

Mae had a mole on her cheek.

CROWE

Now Mae was the red-head ...

LEOPOLD

No, Mae was the brunette.

CROWE

And after this you went home?

LEOPOLD

Correct, Mr. Crowe.

REPORTER 1

Teen Millionaires Named as Suspects!

LOEB

And then Babe brought me home, and that was it. I think that's it. I don't remember anything else of importance on the 21st.

CROWE

And you were in Babe's car the entire time?

LOEB

Right. It's a red Willys-Knight.

CROWE (*To* LEOPOLD)

And you were in your car, the whole day?

LEOPOLD

My car. The whole day.

CROWE

Your red Willys-Knight?

LEOPOLD

Yes, sir.

(CROWE *smiles.*)

REPORTER 1

May 30th, Franks Case Near Conclusion: Leopold/Loeb Under Intense Interrogation!

CROWE

We've got a problem, Nathan. You weren't in your car on the 21st because your chauffeur says he was working on the car all that day.

LEOPOLD

Sven must be mistaken about the date.

CROWE

He was working all day on the car because you wanted him to fix a squeak in the brakes. Isn't that right?

LEOPOLD

Yes, but he must be mistaken about the date.

CROWE

His daughter was ill that day and he had to use your car briefly to take her to the doctor. Don't worry, he asked your father. He has a *dated prescription* from the doctor.

LEOPOLD

Ah.

REPORTER 3

Alibis Under Question; Where were they that day, and what were they doing?

CROWE (*To* LOEB)

So you weren't in Leopold's car—

LOEB

We were, his red—

CROWE

Don't fuck with me, Dick!

LOEB

I—we were in his car—the 21st—I'm sure—

REPORTER 2

May 31st, Leopold And Loeb Cracking Under Pressure?!

CROWE (*To* LEOPOLD, *softly*)

Okay, Babe, here's the thing. Almer Coe and Company sold three very ordinary pairs of glasses last year. Very ordinary glasses with the same prescription lenses. You see, it's not the lenses that are special ... it's the hinges. The hinges on the frames. The hinges for these particular three pairs of glasses were made by the Bobrow Optical Company of Brooklyn, New York. Unique hinges. Lovely unique hinges.

Now three people in Chicago bought these very ordinary glasses with these very unique hinges. One was a man who has been in Europe for the last six months. One was a woman who was wearing her glasses when she opened her door to talk to me. And the third? The third were bought on November 7th, 1923. They cost $11.50.

(*He pulls* LEOPOLD's *glasses from his coat pocket.*)

They were purchased by one Mr. Nathan Leopold, Junior.

(CROWE *places the glasses on* LEOPOLD's *face.*)

CROWE

I think you dropped these.

(*Pause.*)

LEOPOLD

It's over.

ALL THREE REPORTERS

June 1st, Leopold and Loeb Confess!

(*Lights cross fade to...*)

SCENE 12

REPORTER 2

Exclusive to the Herald and Examiner: Leopold's Confession! "The biggest problem was getting a victim. That was left undecided until that day. We decided to take the most likely looking subject that came our way. Bobby Franks happened to be that particular subject."

REPORTER 1

Wednesday, May 21st, 1924.

REPORTER 3

George Lott Pitches Second No-Hit Game of Prep-Season ...

REPORTER 2

Third Volcanic Week: Lillian Gish in "The White Sister" ...

REPORTER 1

Coolidge Tries Chlorine Gas to Dispel Cold ...

REPORTER 3

Marshall Field's Announces Spring White Sale ...

(LEOPOLD *and* LOEB *are center stage in a "car."* LEOPOLD *drives, and* LOEB *sits in the back seat, leaning forward on the front passenger seat as he speaks to* LEOPOLD. *Three plain wooden chairs should be used to suggest the car.*)

LOEB

Just think of it! After months of planning, here we are. Just us. Alone against the hallowed judicial systems of this nation. The audacity I hear you cry! Ah no, simply the natural experimentation of the two supermen, isn't that right, Babe, *Ubermensch*?

LEOPOLD (*Uneasy*)

Right.

LOEB

Damn right! Soon, soon, soon. When this delicious but agonizing suspense is over and we have—make a right here—and we have made our selection and are finally admitted into the pantheon of the gods; that rare and select society that demands violent deeds bravely performed for admission—

LEOPOLD

Look!

LOEB

Johnny Levinson!

(*Silence as they watch and drive.*)

God.

LEOPOLD

Forget it, Dick. There are too many people around. Please—he's too—

LOEB

No. Stop. *Stop*.

(LEOPOLD *stops the car.* LOEB *hops out and crosses downstage to where Levinson is standing and speaks to him—the audience. There is no actor playing Johnny Levinson.*)

LOEB

Hey, Johnny ... Johnny ... How ya' doin'? ... Sure, sure. Hey, do ya want a ride home? My pal and I were just riding past and thought ...

Oh sure. Yeah, of course ... You gonna play at the lot by the Harvard School? ... No, just wondering, yeah, bye.

(LOEB *watches as Levinson continues down the street.*)

Lucky son-of-a-bitch.

(LOEB *hurries back to the car and returns to the back seat.*)

No good. He's set on playing baseball. I suppose we could drive around until he's on his way home from the game and then—

LEOPOLD

That would seem suspicious, don't you think? Just to have been passing twice?

LOEB

Wait. Let me think..

(*Beat.*)

LEOPOLD

This could be the wrong day, you know. Maybe we had better wait until tomorrow or next week—

LOEB

Or next year? Sure.

LEOPOLD

But if no one is around today, what's the use of—

LOEB (*Suddenly inspired*)

We'll wait around the game and see if anyone leaves early!

LEOPOLD

What?

LOEB

We'll wait around the corner from the game and see if someone leaves early. Alone.

LEOPOLD

And then?

LOEB

And then we do it, Babe. Start the car.

(*In silence,* LEOPOLD *starts the car and drives to the lot where the boys are playing baseball.*)

Now, just pull in here, and we can watch the whole game.

(LOEB *never takes his eye off the game—the audience.*)

All right now, we have David Getz at bat. Bobby Franks on first. Little Johnny Swanbeck on third. Phill Kruger—wait, who's that?—Irving Hartmann. Maybe...

(*Pause as* LOEB *watches the game.* LEOPOLD *shifts in his seat.*)

LEOPOLD

And if no one leaves early?

(LOEB *doesn't answer.*)

There are a lot of people around here, Dick. And you talked to Johnny Levinson. Don't you think people might make the connection?

LOEB

Nope.

LEOPOLD

I think it would be better to wait until another day.

LOEB

Do you?

LEOPOLD

It might be better. We don't want to take any undue risks, especially after all the care and planning we've already put into this. We don't want to ruin the whole affair because we were being too hasty—

LOEB

If you're afraid just admit it!

LEOPOLD

I am naturally apprehensive, not afraid.

LOEB (*Coldly*)

Right.

(*Beat.*)

You'll go through with this, and you know why. Because I want you to, dear boy. We have an agreement which constitutes that you will go through with this, and I needn't—

(LOEB, *who has been watching the game, suddenly stiffens. He hisses to* LEOPOLD.)

Bobby Franks is leaving the game!

LEOPOLD

What?

LOEB

Bobby Franks is leaving the game. Alone!

LEOPOLD

Oh God...

LOEB (*With rising passion*)

The little monster is leaving alone. He's walking home. Alone. *Babe, this is it! Start the car. Come on.*

(LEOPOLD *starts the car and begins to follow Bobby Franks.*)

LOEB

Drive slowly. That's it... calm, calm, calm. Just keep calm, old buddy. This is it. This is what we have worked for. Slow down! Just keep calm.

LEOPOLD

Dick...

(LOEB *puts his hand firmly on* LEOPOLD's *shoulder.*)

LOEB (*Soothing*)

Babe.

(*Beat.*)

LEOPOLD

Should I pull up beside him?

LOEB

Right. Nice and slow.

(*The car pulls up next to Bobby Franks, and* LOEB *leans forward and speaks to him through the open front passenger window.*)

Bobby! Bobby Franks! Hiya. Playing a little ball? ... Sure. Hey, Bobby, do ya want a lift home? We're heading right past your house and...

(*Pause as Bobby says no.*)

Sure, okay ... Well, if you say so. See ya later.

(LOEB *is sensing torturous panic and is about to let the whole thing go, when he is suddenly inspired.*)

Bobby! I want to talk to you about that tennis racket! You know, the one I'm working on for you.

(*Beat.* LOEB *smiles warmly.*)

Sure, climb in.

(*They watch as Franks climbs into the front seat. This is mime, there is no actor playing Bobby Franks.*)

Do you mind if we drive around the block? ... Great!

(LOEB *mimes leaning over and picking up a chisel as he chats casually with Bobby Franks.*)

Ah, you see, Bobby, the problem about the racket is that I don't really have the right string so I —

(*Without any warning and with great violence,* LOEB *suddenly smashes Bobby Franks twice over the head with the chisel.* LOEB *lets out a savage, animal scream as he batters Bobby Franks.* LOEB *then drags the body into the back seat and hits him twice more. During this* LEOPOLD *recoils from the blood that has splattered on him and cries out...*)

LEOPOLD

My god!... My god!...

(*After striking the last blow,* LOEB *explodes into giggles as he gasps for breath.*) *Loeb↓*

Calm, calm, calm. Keep calm, old buddy. Watch the road, Babe! Wouldn't want to get into an accident now, would we... might be kind of hard to explain.

(LEOPOLD *pants and cannot speak.*)

LOEB (*Glancing down at the body*)
And within a block of his own home. Ah well, that's life, right?

(*He laughs.*)

(*Beat.* LOEB *looks at* LEOPOLD.)

Really, get a hold of yourself. It's all over just like we planned. In fact, it went better than we planned, right? Everything turned out beautifully, it was a work of art, a work of art.

LEOPOLD (*Finally able to speak*)
Just like swatting a fly.

(*Lights fade on* LEOPOLD *and* LOEB.)

CROWE

Society requires that there be no slipping of the wheels of justice in this case. No home-spun pleading or dramatic elocution can lessen the severity of this crime. It demands that the punishment be meted out with the rigorous impartiality of the old law that recognized no newfangled "mental psychosis." And that old law instructs us: "Thine eye shall not pity, but life shall go for life, eye for eye, tooth for tooth, hand, for hand and foot for foot."

(*Lights cross fade to...*)

SCENE 13

(*A jail ante-room.* LEOPOLD *and* LOEB *together.*
LOEB *reads a newspaper.*)

LOEB

"... Eye for eye, tooth for tooth, hand for hand and foot for foot..."

(*He laughs.*)

Hand for hand, foot for foot, finger for finger.

LEOPOLD

Toothbrush for toothbrush—

LOEB

Cheek to cheek—

LEOPOLD

Tea for two.

(*They laugh.* DARROW *enters.* LEOPOLD *and* LOEB *start and separate.*)

LOEB

Mr. Darrow...

DARROW

Hello, Dick.

LOEB

Mr. Darrow, this is my friend, Nathan Leopold.

DARROW

Nice to meet you, Nathan.

LEOPOLD

It is indeed a profound honor to meet you, Mr. Darrow. I have often remarked to my father of your complex legal arguments and my admiration for the mechanics of your mind.

LOEB

You will be defending us, sir?

DARROW

Yes.

I can't tell you how happy I am you decided to take our case!

(*To* LEOPOLD)

Mr. Darrow is an old friend of the family. He's known me forever ...

LEOPOLD

That's nice.

LOEB

Sure, all seems a bit more pleasant that way. At least we can depend on him. Right, Mr. Darrow? And it sure looks as if we're going to need the best—

DARROW

Now hold on a minute, Dick.

LOEB

Mr. Darrow?

(*Beat.*)

DARROW

Did you boys kill Bobby Franks?

LOEB (*Matter-of-fact*)

Oh yes.

(*Beat.*)

DARROW

My God ... *Why?*

LEOPOLD (*Snide*)

I don't think you'd understand.

(DARROW *sets down his briefcase and sits.*) *in the chair*

DARROW

Try me.

(*Lights cross fade to...*)

SCENE 14

(LEOPOLD *and* LOEB *stand.* "What'll I Do," *a mournful song of the period, begins to play. Both listen.* LEOPOLD *and* LOEB *circle each other in a vaguely predatory manner. They stop.*)

(*As the music swells they come together and begin to dance. They dance round the stage in a slow, perfect waltz.*)

(*When the songs ends, they stop.*)

LOEB

Of course we could do it.

(*Blackout.*)

ACT 2

SCENE 15

(*Lights come up on* LEOPOLD *and* LOEB. *They are on the marshes, having just put Bobby Franks' body into a culvert.* LOEB *wanders with typical nervous energy—busy cleaning himself, wiping blood and mud from his clothes.* LEOPOLD *stands still, looking down at the body. There is no actor or prop to suggest the body.* LEOPOLD *does not look away from the body until the end of the scene.*)

LOEB

Christ, I hate mud! I'm gonna have to throw this suit away now. You're not too muddy are you?

LEOPOLD

No.

LOEB

I love this suit, too. Well, serves me right—I should have worn that tatty old serge thing. So, we've got to put the address on the ransom note now and get that in the mail to the Franks. We won't need the phone books, cause I know the address—

LEOPOLD (*Still looking at the body*)
The acid didn't work.

(LOEB *glances down at the body for a moment as he passes and then moves off.*)

LOEB

No, not really. We should have used sulfuric, like I said. Doesn't matter, though, no one is going to find him in this godforsaken spot.

LEOPOLD

Desolate.

LOEB

Hm?

LEOPOLD

It's desolate here. The marshes.

LOEB

Very. Anyway—home to change—address the ransom note and mail it—dump his clothes—return the car—get rid of this gorgeous suit, much as that will pain me—then make the call to the Franks' tomorrow. Everything's right on track.

LEOPOLD

I tasted his blood.

LOEB

What?

LEOPOLD

When you did it. His blood splashed on my face. I tasted his blood.

LOEB

What did it taste like?

    (*Beat.*)

LEOPOLD

Metallic.

    (*Beat.*)

LOEB

Was it warm?

LEOPOLD

It was hot.

(*Beat.*)

LOEB

Okay, boy-o, let's get cracking, we've got buckets to do—

LEOPOLD

Dick ... just stand here for a minute.

(LOEB *stops. Beat.*)

LEOPOLD

Come here. Stand here with me.

(LOEB *moves to* LEOPOLD. *They look down at the body.*)

(*Pause.*)

(LEOPOLD *looks at* LOEB *for the first time in the scene.*)

LEOPOLD

We really did this.

LOEB

We did.

LEOPOLD

There's no going back. We're together now. Forever.

(*Beat.*)

(LOEB *looks down at the body.*)

LOEB (*Simply*)

Next time, I wanna taste the blood.

(*Lights cross fade to...*)

SCENE 16

(The courtroom.)

REPORTER 3

July 21, 1924. Leopold And Loeb Trial Begins Today!

REPORTER 1

Chicago Demands Death!

REPORTER 1 2

Never Has Public Opinion Been at Such a White Heat of Indignation!

REPORTER 1

State's Attorney Robert Crowe nervously stalked the courtroom floor like a hungry tiger smelling blood.

REPORTER 2

While Defense Attorney Clarence Darrow had a leisurely and pacific chat with his infamous clients.

REPORTER 3

Courtroom Temperature Climbs to ninety-nine Degrees. "Sure Is Hot," Says Loeb.

REPORTER 1

All the while the razor-sharp Crowe and the hang-dog Darrow faced off like opposing armies, primed for battle.

REPORTER 3

At last all is silent and the Trial of the Century is suddenly upon us...

BAILIFF

The People of the State of Illinois versus Nathan Leopold, Jr and Richard Loeb for the crime of murder, before the Honorable

Judge John R. Caverly, in the Criminal Court of Cook County, at the July term A.D. 1924. All rise.

DARROW (*Stands and addresses
the judge—the audience*)
Your Honor, before the selection of the jury I have a motion.

CROWE (*Stands*)
Your Honor, I must object.

(*To* DARROW)

You couldn't wait for your opening statement, Clarence?

DARROW
Oh, I think you'll want to hear this, Bob.

(*He turns forward.*)

Your Honor, my clients would like to change their plea to "Guilty."

(*The courtroom explodes. The reporters whisper excitedly, scribble notes, etc.*)

CROWE
Now hold on a minute—you're changing your pleas?

DARROW
Guilty on all counts.

CROWE
This is extraordinary!

DARROW
Well, this is an extraordinary case.

CROWE
This is a standard trial for murder, nothing more.

DARROW

No, Bob, I believe I've just turned it into a sentencing hearing.

CROWE

You're out of your mind.

DARROW

Maybe so.

(CROWE *tosses a book down on his desk*.)

Now, Bob, don't get mad.

CROWE

Your Honor, I must protest at the Counsel for the Defense's melodramatic tactics—

DARROW

Why? It's kosher. We're just changing our pleas.

CROWE

So, what, you suddenly decided they were guilty?

DARROW

Your Honor, I suppose we can release the jury candidates now.

(CROWE *sits*.)

BAILIFF

A plea of guilty being so entered no jury has been called. The Honorable Judge John R. Caverly presiding and sentencing.

(DARROW *shambles forward*.)

DARROW

Your Honor, my clients and I decided to change our plea to "guilty." Now, I'm not going to be coy with you, in doing so we have removed the jury from these proceedings. In doing so we have placed the responsibility for assigning the punishment of these two boys firmly on your shoulders. It is now entirely up to you as to where their future lies. If these boys are to stand on the gallows and plunge to a *sharp, choking death,* it will be your decision. And your decision alone.

Now, in the course of this hearing we will produce a number of expert witnesses who will testify as to the psychological state of my clients before, during, and after their crime. It is my—

CROWE (*Stands*)

Is the Counsel for the Defense going to suggest that they were insane at the time of the crime? Because if he is, then Illinois law requires that we must call a jury.

DARROW (*To* CROWE)

I'm not going to suggest that.

CROWE (*To* DARROW)

Then I'm not sure as to the purpose of introducing this psychological testimony.

DARROW

Your Honor, I'm going to present testimony as to my clients' mental state that will serve to explain—not justify—but explain their actions. I believe we must begin to look beyond the horror of the crime as we try to remember the difficult, treacherous road that separates childhood from maturity. It is my belief that it is primary to the rendering of punishment that we understand their *motivations.* To do so we must begin, of course, with a complete understanding of their psychological health.

CROWE

Now it seems to me that the Counsel for the Defense is just begging the question. He doesn't want to call them insane—cause then we'd have to call a jury—but he wants to make them just insane enough to reduce culpability and get a lighter sentence.

DARROW (*To* CROWE)

On the continuum of mental health there are a great many levels between sane and insane.

CROWE (*To* DARROW)

And in a court of law there are not. If they knew what they were doing was wrong, then they are sane. Pure and simple. We needn't muddy the waters with—

DARROW (*To* CROWE)

The darkest recesses of the human mind are in question here. We must take that fact into account to arrive at a just verdict of punishment.

CROWE

Well, it seems to me that the Counsel for the Defense is just afraid of a jury, so he pleads them "guilty." But he's afraid to call them "insane" cause that means we gotta have one. I wonder why the Counsel for the Defense so fears the opinion of the good people of Chicago? Is it because the will of the people is so very clear in this case? Their verdict has been rendered on every street of this city day after day. Their verdict will not be denied by my worthy opponent. Their verdict—

DARROW

Well, if the State's Attorney would resist the temptation to sway this court during *my opening statement*, perhaps we'll actually get to some damn verdict in the next year or so!

CROWE

But—to my knowledge—which is considerable—

DARROW

Yes, it is.

CROWE

To my knowledge, psychological testimony has never been admitted into a court of law as a mitigating circumstance when a defendant has pled guilty.

DARROW

Well, as my old Daddy used to say, "Even Davy Crockett killed his first bear somewhere."

REPORTER 1

Darrow Pleads Them Guilty!

REPORTER 3

Darrow Runs from Jury! City Outraged!

REPORTER 2

Wily old Clarence Darrow has done it again. As the people of Chicago have been enjoying the thought of finally putting the noose around the loathsome necks of Leopold and Loeb, Big Bad Clarence Darrow has come in to rain on the party. Now the citizens of Chicago will be denied their right to affix the punishment of death to these heartless "supermen." But foxy Mr. Darrow might be outfoxed yet, as Judge Caverly is popularly known as a "Hanging Judge." Oh, what will poor Mr. Darrow do now?

(*Lights cross fade to...*)

SCENE 17

(LEOPOLD *and* LOEB. *A jail ante-room. They are reading various newspaper accounts of the trial.* LOEB *laughs.*)

LOEB

Look at this one!

(*He shows a picture in the paper to* LEOPOLD.)

LEOPOLD

The cat's meow.

LOEB (*Reads*)

"... To this reporter's eye it seems inconceivable in the extreme that this good-looking golden boy could have committed..." etcetera, etcetera.

LEOPOLD (*Handing* LOEB *another paper*)
Gander at this, golden-boy.

LOEB
"Richard Loeb, whose winning smile has captured many an eye during this hearing, watched the proceedings with a studied air of *insouciance*..." Boy, read 'em and weep.

LEOPOLD
How come I always look so fishy in the pictures?

LOEB
Actually, you look more like a bug here.

LEOPOLD
Thanks.

LOEB
You know, when we get off I think I'm going to star in the flickers. Can't you just see it, Babe? Me on the screen, thirty feet high, pitching the woo to Mary Pickford. Or better yet—*Theda Bara*!

Man oh man, this is great! Here we are at last, Babe, on top if it all. While all the rest—while all the insects—

LEOPOLD
All the ants.

LOEB
Gaze up at us in horror and profound wonder.

LEOPOLD
Blinded by our light.

LOEB
I mean, did you see all the girls lined up in front of the court? Swooning like we were John Gilbert or something.

Oh, I got this today!

(*He hands a note to* LEOPOLD.)

One of the bailiffs slipped it to me on the sly.

LEOPOLD (*Reads*)

"Dear Dick,

"I have watched you day after day in the court and the time has
come to speak of my love for you. You are the swellest guy—"
Swellest? "You are the swellest guy I've ever seen with your
dreamy eyes... " How come I never get love notes?

LOEB

Cause you're so buggy.

(LEOPOLD *sees something in one of the newspapers and laughs.*)

LEOPOLD

Oh my God!

LOEB

What? What?

(LEOPOLD *hands the paper to* LOEB. LOEB *reads.*)

REPORTER 2

Dickie Needs Love. The Enquirer Asks: Would You Go Out with
"Angel Face" Dickie Loeb?

LOEB

Oh no!

REPORTER 2

All female applicants between the ages of eighteen and twenty-
four are invited to answer the question below and return it to
The Enquirer on or before August Tenth: "Why Would You Like
a Date with Richard Loeb?" Please restrict your answers to fifty
words or less.

LOEB

Fifty words or less! They've got to be kidding!

LEOPOLD

They could just write "Because he's just the swellest, swellest, swellest" fifty times!

(LOEB *has noticed something in a paper*.)

LOEB (*Seriously*)

Babe, look at this.

REPORTER 1

Chicago Tribune, Rumor Has It That Mrs. Franks Has Gone Mad.

REPORTER 3

One of the many victims of this crime has been Mrs. Flora Franks, mother of young Bobby Franks. Unable to accept her son's death, she insists that he is still alive and is being hidden...

REPORTER 1

A haunted and beguiled figure, she listlessly roams the halls of her great house asking, "When will Bobby return?"

(*Beat*.)

LOEB (*Simply*)

Never.

(*Lights cross fade to...*)

SCENE 18

(*The courtroom.* CROWE *is examining* SERGEANT GORTLAND *on the witness stand.* DARROW *appears to be asleep at his table.* LEOPOLD *and* LOEB *talk quietly between themselves.*)

REPORTER 3

Dr. William McNally, chemist; Dr. John Wassner, chemist; Dr. Ralph Webster, chemist...

REPORTER 2

Roger Abbey, journalist; Dr. Paul Campbell Edwards, taxidermist; Percy Van Bogert, pharmacy owner...

REPORTER 3

James Kemp, clerk; George Lewis, ornithologist; Alvin Goldstein, police officer; Lawrence Cuneo, attorney....

REPORTER 2

Over One Hundred Witnesses Called by the State.

REPORTER 3

Frank Mullina, police officer; William O'Hare, police officer; James Gortland, police officer...

CROWE

Now, Sergeant Gortland, you were in charge of guarding Nathan Leopold after his arrest?

GORTLAND

Yes.

CROWE

And in that time did he speak to you about the crime?

GORTLAND

Yes.

CROWE

Can you tell us specifically some of the things you talked about?

GORTLAND

Well, at one point I asked him, "What do you think your defense will be?"

(DARROW *raises his head, suddenly alert.*)

GORTLAND

And he says to me, "I guess I will plead guilty and hopefully get a *soft judge* who will not hang me but give me life imprisonment—"

DARROW (*Quickly to* LEOPOLD)

Did you say that, Babe?

LEOPOLD

Certainly not!

GORTLAND

"I have a lot of things I want to do," he says, "which I feel would be of benefit to mankind."

CROWE

Thank you, Sergeant Gortland, I have no further questions.

(CROWE *returns to his table and sits.* DARROW *stands and moves in on* GORTLAND *quickly, his voice cold and his questions very sharp and fast.*)

DARROW

Sergeant Gortland, where did you have this *alleged* conversation with Nathan Leopold?

GORTLAND (*Startled*)

In ... in a jail ante-room.

DARROW

Did you tell anyone else about this conversation?

GORTLAND

Uh... no...

DARROW

No?

GORTLAND

No—I mean yes—

DARROW

Which is it, boy?

GORTLAND

I told my wife.

DARROW

When?

GORTLAND

Uh... last Monday—*Sunday*.

DARROW

Oh, I see! You've said nothing about this alleged conversation for two months and then you suddenly told it to someone just three days ago?

GORTLAND (*With a quick glance to* CROWE)

Yes—I mean no!

(DARROW *shifts his position to block* GORTLAND's *view of* CROWE.)

DARROW

Isn't that peculiar.

GORTLAND

Well—

DARROW

Do you know what perjury means, sonny?

GORTLAND

Um, yes...

DARROW

What made you change your mind three days ago about the importance of this conversation?

GORTLAND

I... I...

DARROW

Did you make any notes of this conversation?

GORTLAND

Yes!

DARROW

Where are those notes?

GORTLAND

In my notebook.

DARROW

Well, that follows. Do you have that notebook? Let me see it.

GORTLAND

This is it...

(GORTLAND *hands a small notebook to* DARROW.)

DARROW

Ah...

(DARROW *flips through the notebook and wanders.*)

"Lunch, eighty-five cents... Taxi fare, a dollar thirty-five... Take Fuzzy in for shots—" Who's Fuzzy?

GORTLAND

My dog.

DARROW

Uh-huh.

(*Beat as* DARROW continues to flip through the book.)

GORTLAND

He's a dachshund.

DARROW

Good for him.

(DARROW *suddenly stops flipping through the book.*)

Is this it? Is *this* the note you made? "If not hang plead guilty." Is *that all?*

GORTLAND

Uh... yes...

DARROW

And *where* does it say anything about pleading guilty before a "*soft judge*"?

(GORTLAND *stammers nervously.*)

DARROW

Isn't it a fact that Nathan Leopold never said that? Isn't it a fact that you said it here today because you were *coached* to do it?

CROWE (*Jumping to his feet*)

Your Honor, I object!

DARROW

Isn't it nothing but a low-down lie?

(*The court erupts into action. The reporters stand and scribble notes madly.* DARROW *and* CROWE *shout at each other simultaneously*)

CROWE

This is out of the question! You are harassing this witness! I object to this blatant disregard for the right of the...

DARROW

I don't know how you can come into a court of law with nonsense like this! Your case has stretched out over a month now, but this...

(LEOPOLD *and* LOEB *laugh as the panic continues and the* *lights cross fade to...*) Move offstage

SCENE 19

(*The courtroom. It is the ending of the day in court. The* *reporters and* LEOPOLD *and* LOEB *move away.* DARROW *is* *just leaving the courtroom when...*)

CROWE

Clarence, can I talk to you for a second?

DARROW

Yes, Bob.

(*Beat.*)

(*Simultaneously*)

CROWE

I just want to say—

DARROW

Look, I really have—

(*Beat.*)

CROWE

Go ahead, please.

DARROW

No, you go.

CROWE

Well, Clarence, I know you think I'm being hard on these boys...

(DARROW *does not respond.*)

And I am.

DARROW (*Coldly*)

That's your job.

CROWE

Yes, but I know how you feel. I really don't have to justify anything to you, but—

DARROW (*Turning to go*)

Then don't bother.

CROWE

Why are you so angry?

DARROW

We pled *guilty* to the crime, Bob. Calling all these witnesses to rehash the events is beneath contempt! We don't have a jury. I don't know who you're trying to impress—

CROWE

Now don't you get all saintly on me, Clarence. You have selfish motives too.

DARROW

Go to hell.

(*He starts to go.*)

CROWE

Why'd you take this case?

(DARROW *stops.*)

A nice big public forum for your ideas—

DARROW

Yeah, my "anarchistic ideas," I read that, Bob.

CROWE

So all the reporters go away writing about Mr. Darrow. I'll tell you, I could use that press.

DARROW

I didn't take this case for the press.

CROWE

Yeah, what the hell do you need with good press? I mean, you're Clarence Darrow, world-famous lawyer. But I'm just What's-His-Name State's Attorney. And all that people are gonna remember when they go into the voting box is whether I did what they want. And they want to hang Leopold and Loeb.

DARROW

So you wanna hang these boys to get votes?

CROWE

No. I am following the will of this city.

DARROW

What the hell can you possibly know about the will of the city? What do you see from your office up there on the forty-fourth floor?

CROWE

Look, you can afford to posture your way through this hearing. You can afford to be all dramatic and philanthropic. You can afford to take your time and—

DARROW

You have called one hundred and two witnesses to the stand, my friend! That's taking your time!

CROWE

And all the while Mr. Darrow just shambles along making his little points for humanity.

DARROW

I believe in what I say up there!

CROWE

And so do I!

DARROW

Bullshit!

CROWE

What the hell gives you the right—

DARROW

And all that crap about pleading guilty before a "soft judge"—

CROWE

I believe what I say up there! They are guilty and deserve to die. Period. And if we don't hang them we will be mocking justice— just like they do every day in this court.

DARROW

They're boys, Bob. *Boys*. And they're scared.

CROWE

Come on, what do you want? You want to throw away the law? If we do that, what will we have left? What will *we* stand for, Clarence? You know what's happening in Chicago. You know about the gangs and corruption. It's just creeping in. Everywhere. All because the laws are not being enforced! You like that? I want my children to grow up in a city where they can depend on the law to protect them. So they can depend on at least that. So if everything else just falls to shit, at least they'll know there's *justice somewhere*.

DARROW

"Justice"? Hanging these two boys is gonna give us justice?

CROWE

It's a start.

DARROW

Well, Bob, we've done a hell of a lot of hanging and we're no closer to justice than ever before.

CROWE

It's the *law*, Clarence. You may not like it much but we *hang* killers in Chicago.

DARROW

I have never had a client executed and I'm not going to let you hang these boys.

CROWE

Ah, so there it is: Clarence Darrow's famous *reputation*. Wouldn't want to fuck up your perfect score, right?

DARROW

You're a cold bastard.

CROWE

And you are a blind old man.

(*Pause.*)

DARROW

I could look at them like you do, Bob. I could damn these boys for what they did. For the madness, for the brutality...
    I can see the sin in all the world.
    And I may well hate that sin, but never the sinner.

(*Beat.*)

CROWE

And I wonder what Mrs. Franks would say to that?

(*Lights cross fade to...*)

SCENE 20

(LEOPOLD *and* LOEB *in jail cells.*)

LOEB

Dear Mom and Pop,

This thing is all too terrible.

LEOPOLD

Dear Father,

Thank you for the books.

LOEB

I have thought and thought about it and even now I just cannot figure out how it all came about. Of one thing I am certain, though, and that is that I have no one to blame but myself.

LEOPOLD

I have been starved for challenging reading material, so I tore into your recent shipment with great eagerness.

LOEB

I am afraid you two may try to blame yourselves for what happened. Please, please don't.

LEOPOLD

I was particularly excited to receive, and have been most stimulated by, Professor Branson's *Phrenology of Ornithologia.* It is a truly fascinating study of the skeletal structure of birds, with particular attention to the cranial development of various species.

LOEB

At best I know I have a long prison term staring at me, but I am hopeful that someday I shall be free again and I really and truly think I shall be able to do the world some good and at least try to live a much better life than I have.

LEOPOLD

It had been my expectation that what we commonly consider to the be the higher order of fowl—such as hawks and falcons—would have markedly the largest brain pans and cranial cavities. Interestingly, however, the order *Icteridae*, the common black-bird, has a proportionally much larger skull than, for example, the peregrine falcon.

LOEB

What I really wanted to tell you is that I am not as hard-hearted as I am appearing. Of course, dearest ones, I am afraid my heart is not what it should be, or how could I have done what I did?

LEOPOLD (*Softly*)

Not that it much matters, I suppose, as I will certainly never see a falcon again.

LOEB

Your son,

Dick.

LEOPOLD

Yours sincerely,

Nathan.

LOEB

P.S. Mother dear, still no word from you. I don't know if you're planning to come to town for any of the trial...it could not possibly do any good although I should *dearly* love to see you...

(*Lights cross fade to...*)

SCENE 21

REPORTER 1
June 7th: Are They Sane? Fathers Ask.

CROWE
Mrs. Darrow Found Leopold And Loeb "Very Polite."

REPORTER 1
July 17th...

REPORTER 2
The Chicago Tribune offers a fabulous opportunity for its readers to witness the inner workings of our most sacred halls of justice. We ask our readers: should we radio broadcast the Leopold and Loeb trial?

REPORTER 1
Ballots can be found on page three.

REPORTER 2
Please send us your response!

REPORTER 1
Your votes decide!

(*The courtroom.* GERMAINE RHEINHARDT *takes the witness chair. She is chewing gum and looking about.*)

REPORTER 3
July 29th: State Quizzes Girl Who Found Loeb "The Nicest Boy, Really."

(GERMAINE *is responding to a question from* CROWE.)

GERMAINE (*With captivating energy*)
It was Friday night, a few days after the murder, the... Twenty-third? Yeah, that's right. So anyways, we went to dinner and then

dancing. Dick was always a great dancer, he really knew how to cover the floor, real smooth. That Friday night we were dancing in a big crowd at the Edgewater Beach Club. We started really moving and dipping and spinning and everything, and pretty soon the whole dance floor was ours, and all the other couples were just standing round the edge just watchin' us. They were mostly older and not too good dancers, ya know? I really felt kinda special being there with Dick, who is the nicest boy, really. We musta made quite a sight; when the music stopped, we ended in one of those big swirls leading into a final dip, real dramatic. Anyway, all the other couples applauded afterwards, and Dick made us take this big bow—

(CROWE *finally cuts in.*)

CROWE

Miss Rheinhardt, were you Richard Loeb's only girl friend?

GERMAINE

Well, no, I guess not. I knew Dick was seein' lots of other girls, but I always felt I was number one. And I don't see any of them other girls here. Only me. And even if Dick was going out with other girls, I always felt I was his special girl, and as long as I felt really special I didn't—

CROWE

Miss Rheinhardt, please stay to exact testimony, things that really happened.

GERMAINE (*Embarrassed*)

Oh... oh sure. Sorry.

CROWE

It's quite all right. Now, did you notice anything peculiar about Richard Loeb's behavior that Friday night following the murder?

GERMAINE

Well, after we danced we went for a drive. We drove up north to one of those beaches overlooking the lake ... it was very romantic and we started, well, fooling around, ya know—

CROWE

Did you have sexual relations with Richard Loeb?

(GERMAINE *reacts as if she has been slapped.*)

(*Pause.*)

Miss Rheinhardt, did you have sexual relations with Richard Loeb?

GERMAINE

No.

CROWE

That night?

GERMAINE

No.

CROWE

Before that at any point?

(*Beat.*)

GERMAINE

No.

CROWE

Ah.

(*Beat.*)

Go on, Miss Rheinhardt, about Richard Loeb's behavior that Friday night after the murder.

GERMAINE (*Head down*)

Well, he was kinda quiet after we left the club. Very quiet. Which is unusual for Dick. He's usually chattering on about something—baseball, money, school, anything. He sure could talk a girl...

(*Beat.*)

But that night he was real quiet. We sat in his car and looked out over the lake, which was real pretty on account of the moonlight. He had his arm around me, and we just sat there. It got sad after a while. Just sad... When I asked Dick to take me home he said, I remember this, he just whispered it: "Don't leave me now, I don't want to be alone, and I'm so afraid of the dark." That's all.

(*Lights cross fade to...*)

SCENE 22

(*Jail Cells.* LEOPOLD *and* LOEB *are in separate cells. A reporter is with each.*)

REPORTER 1:

Nathan, I just feel sorry for you—

LEOPOLD

Now listen, I don't want that. I don't feel sorry for what I did, I did it and that's all. Besides, with our looks and Darrow's brains, I figure we'll do all right.

REPORTER 1

Has your opinion of Dick changed since your imprisonment?

(*Beat.*)

LEOPOLD

Not at all.

REPORTER 1

Nathan, do you feel any remorse?

LEOPOLD

I can't see why.

REPORTER 1

Not even for Mrs. Franks?

LEOPOLD

Every member of the Franks family could drop dead right now, and I wouldn't give a damn. There was no animosity towards the Franks ever. The killing was an experiment. It is just as easy to justify such a death as to justify an entomologist in killing a beetle on a pin!

(*Beat.*)

Now beat it, I've got work to do.

REPORTER 1

Sure. See ya in court.

LEOPOLD

Right.

(REPORTER 1 *goes.*)

LEOPOLD

Has my opinion of Dick changed ... ?

(*Beat.*)

I can illustrate that by saying that I feel myself less than dust beneath his feet. I am jealous of the food and water he takes because I cannot come as close to him as food and water do. I know he doesn't deserve my adoration. I know, but I don't care. More and more I begin to understand that there is something ... *hollow* ... inside him. Something lonely, lost ... cold. But to me he is like a hard, perfect gem—hold him to the light and turn him slowly in your hand and the different dazzling facets will catch your eye and fascinate you one after another. How could I ever hope to escape from that blinding light? That flashing, glimmering brilliance that reflects on me ... and makes me beautiful too.

LOEB (*To* REPORTER 3)

I know I should be sorry I killed that young boy and all, but I just don't feel it. That's why I could do it, I suppose, nothing inside to stop me.

REPORTER 3

Dick, the folks on the outside think you're about the coldest-blooded mortal in the world because of the way you act in court. You laugh, you josh, you appear to be having a fine time.

LOEB

Well, how do they want me to act?

REPORTER 3

I don't know, behave with less bravado, act natural.

LOEB

That's exactly what I am doing. I sit in the courtroom and watch the play. When the crowd laughs, I laugh. When it's time to be serious, I'm that way too. Mostly. I've watched you in the courtroom, Dennis, and you laugh and smile and yawn and look bored, and so do all the others. Why should I be any different?

REPORTER 3

You just don't seem terribly concerned about the trial.

LOEB

Why should I be? What can I do? In some ways it's great, I mean here I am, the criminal mastermind. Everyone stares when I enter a room. They whisper. They're afraid. People look where I look. They suspend when I speak. They wait, breathless...

Besides, this thing will be the making of me! I'll spend a few years in jail, and then I'll be released. I'll come out to a new life!

(*Beat.* REPORTER 3 *stares at* LOEB, *speechless.*)

REPORTER 3

Well ... thanks for the interview, Dick.

LOEB (*With a winning smile*)

Sure thing.

(REPORTER 3 *exits. Pause.*)

LOEB (*Softly and seriously*)

And you know, Teddy...

REPORTER 1

July 25th, Slayers Spurn Sympathy!

REPORTER 3

Loeb Hears Self Dissected In Court.

REPORTER 2

July 27th, Hypnotism May Play Role in Leopold/ Loeb Defense.

REPORTER 3

Alienist Attests Leopold Has "Mesmeric Powers"!

REPORTER 2

Could He Have Put His Crime Partner into a Trance for the Committing of the Gruesome Crime?

REPORTER 1

July Twenty-ninth, 1924. Mother Abandons Dickie!

REPORTER 3

Mrs. Albert Loeb, mother of Richard Loeb, will not return to Chicago to stand by the side of her boy on trial for his life...

LOEB (*Again, softly and seriously*)
And you know, Teddy...

LEOPOLD
In one sense he's the greatest enemy I'll ever have. My friend-
ship with him could well cost me my life.

LOEB (*Quietly*)
I am small, my heart is pure...

LEOPOLD
But I guess that's not so much to pay. Not so much at all.

(*Lights cross fade to...*)

SCENE 23

(LEOPOLD *and* LOEB *sit. They are watching
a baseball game in the jail yard.*)

REPORTER 2
Weeping Girls Mourn Plight of Richard Loeb.

REPORTER 1
August 3rd, Twenty-four-Hour Watch on Slayers: Elite of Jail
Think Leopold "Ain't So Much."

REPORTER 3
Richard Loeb has adjusted well to prison routine, taking active
part in the frequent baseball games in the "bull pen" while
Nathan Leopold shuns prison routine and society...

LOEB (*Gesturing and
calling to a player*)
That means splitter—he's gonna throw a split—watch his hand!

(*He laughs.*)

The one with the ball, you moron!

LEOPOLD

You're sure you don't want to play?

LOEB

No, I'd rather talk to you. I barely get to see you anymore outside of court. It would do you good to play, though, might get rid
of some of that ghastly pallor.

LEOPOLD

I'm very proud of my ghastly pallor.

LOEB

So how do you think it's going?

LEOPOLD

I really don't know much about baseball.

LOEB

No, I mean the trial, you numbskull.

LEOPOLD

Oh. Inconclusive, thus far. The summations will decide it. I'm
just glad we don't have a jury.

LOEB

Me too.

LEOPOLD

Pretty savvy of Mr. Darrow, don't you think?

(*Beat.*)

LOEB

How's your cell?

LEOPOLD

Too far from yours.

(LOEB *smiles.*)

LOEB

It's not so bad here, really. The guys are good eggs, and the food's okay. The baseball games are fun.

LEOPOLD

You are more adaptable than am I.

LOEB

I guess so. I miss my Mom. Not that she deserves it, the stupid old cow. You know she's not coming to town to see me? And I still haven't heard a word from her. Can you believe that? *Not one word.* I guess I'm ... disowned.

(*Beat. Then he calls to a player*)

Hey, McCabe, you're swinging too soon! The ball's not gonna hurt you, ya sissy!

(*He laughs.*)

I wouldn't want to spend my whole life here.

LEOPOLD

Don't worry, you won't have to, in either case. If they don't hang us they'll send us to a state prison. I'm hoping for Stateville. It has the largest prison library in the state.

LOEB (*Smiles*)

You've researched this, of course.

LEOPOLD

Of course. Stateville's the place. I hope at least one of us goes there.

LOEB

What do you mean?

LEOPOLD

Well, they're not going to keep us together.

LOEB

What?

LEOPOLD

Come on, Dick, they're going to split us up eventually. You didn't think they were going to send us to the prison, did you?

LOEB

Sure I did.

(*Beat.*)

LEOPOLD (*Gently*)

No, I doubt it.

(*Beat.*)

LOEB

I never thought about that.

(*Beat.*)

Isn't that funny? I never thought they might break up. Guess that makes me a dope.

(*Pause.*)

If they hang us—would they do that together? At same time?

LEOPOLD

Probably. They have two gallows here, side by side.

LOEB

Then I hope they hang us.

(*Beat. Then* LOEB *calls to a player*)

What did I tell you—splitter! Are you blind? I said watch his goddamn hands!

(*Beat.*)

LEOPOLD

Mr. Darrow's doing a fine job.

LOEB

You think too much of him.

LEOPOLD

Do I?

LOEB

Yes, you do.

He's just another one of the insects after all. Just another old man shouting his morality at us. At the two *Ubermensch*, right?

LEOPOLD

I think you're wrong.

LOEB

Wrong?

LEOPOLD

He's more than that.

LOEB

Come on, don't be a sucker, Babe.

LEOPOLD

That's what I think.

(*Beat.*)

(LEOPOLD *watches a bird flying past high above them.* LOEB *watches him.*)

(*Pause.*)

LOEB

You miss it, don't you?

LEOPOLD

What?

LOEB

The outside.

LEOPOLD

More than I ever thought I would. And the funny thing is that I miss the oddest things: elevated trains, that tree outside my window that used to scare me when I was a kid. And the birds.

LOEB

Mm.

LEOPOLD

Mostly the birds, I guess. What about you? What do you miss?

(*Beat.*)

LOEB

Nothing.

(*Beat.*)

LOEB (*Calling to a player*)
Come on, Hayes, it was a mile outside the box—go for the walk!

LEOPOLD

Dick, really, go play if you want. I'm happy watching.

LOEB (*Not looking at* LEOPOLD)
No, I want to stay with you.

(*Pause.*)

(*Lights cross-fade to:*)

SCENE 24

REPORTER 1
August 14th, Chicago Tribune. Leopold and Loeb: Nuts or Not?

REPORTER 3
Head-Doctor's Third Day on Stand!

REPORTER 2
Darrow's Final Witness Paints Lurid Picture of Lethal Crime-Twins.

(*The courtroom.* DARROW *stands examining* DR. WHITE *on the stand.*)

DARROW
And how would you judge the boys' emotional development?

WHITE
Arrested. Arrested emotional development. Intellectually they are both highly advanced. Babe, in particular demonstrates an academic voraciousness that I have rarely seen. Indeed, at times I wasn't sure who was interviewing whom!

DARROW (*With a wry look to* LEOPOLD)
I know the feeling.

WHITE
But despite this intelligence, I would judge their emotional development—the process of their natural maturation—to have been arrested somewhere under the age of ten.

DARROW
You mean they are less developed than ten year olds?

WHITE

Yes. They seem to exist in an ego-centered universe that allows only for hedonistic expressions designed to satisfy their primal urges for dominance which—

DARROW

Whoa, Doctor White, please remember I'm just an old country bumpkin. Could you give it to me a little more plain?

WHITE

Well, simply put, I don't think Babe would have committed a crime by himself because he had not the criminalistic tendencies that Dickie did. And I don't think Dickie would ever have functioned to this criminal extent by himself without someone to support and encourage him. The psychiatric cause for the crime is not to be found in either boy *alone*, but in the interweaving of their peculiarly interdigited personalities.

DARROW

Thank you, Dr. White. Now I assume Mr. Crowe has some questions for you.

(DARROW *goes to his table, sits.* CROWE *stands and walks to* WHITE.)

CROWE

Dr. White, we certainly appreciate the time and effort and *expense*, which is evident, that our distinguished Counsel for the Defense has put into all these alienists and this careful analysis. We appreciate, Dr. White, your time and effort. But in all this testimony I somehow missed a thing or two. Could you answer one little question for me, Dr. White?

WHITE

Surely.

CROWE

Thank you. Dr. White, are they insane?

WHITE

I don't think I've thought about the matter.

CROWE

I beg your pardon?

WHITE

Sane and insane are legal terms, not medical ones.

CROWE

Dr. White, when I am in your park, I'll play by your rules. When you are in a court of law you are obliged, to the best of your ability, to play by our rules.

WHITE

Very well.

CROWE

Are they insane?

WHITE

I have not thought about the matter.

(*Beat.* CROWE *gives* DR. WHITE *a stony stare.*)

CROWE

Did they know what they were doing was wrong?

WHITE

Oh yes.

CROWE

So they were fully responsible for their actions?

WHITE

No, I wouldn't say that.

CROWE

Well who the hell was responsible then, Sigmund Freud?

DARROW (*Standing*)

I needn't point out to Mr. Crowe that since he lives in Vienna, Sigmund Freud is not under suspicion in this particular case.

(*Beat.*)

CROWE

Now, Dr. White, when you were making your examinations, did you ask Nathan Leopold who actually struck the blows that killed Bobby Franks?

WHITE

No, I don't think I did.

CROWE

Well, have you any opinion as to who killed Bobby Franks?

WHITE

Yes, I believe Dickie did it.

(*A press explosion.*)

REPORTER 1

Witness Declares "Dickie Did It!"

REPORTER 2

For the first time in these proceedings, a witness has expressed the opinion that *Richard Loeb* struck the blows that killed little Bobby Franks ...

REPORTER 3

His face pale and his shoulders hunched, Richard Loeb hurried out of the courtroom—

REPORTER 2

And suddenly the self-assured young charmer was a furtive killer.

(*Lights cross fade to...*)

SCENE 25

(The jail anteroom. LOEB *pursues* LEOPOLD.*)*

LOEB

At least think about it!

LEOPOLD

No!

LOEB

At least read the statement.

(LEOPOLD *stops and* LOEB *hands him a piece of paper.*
LEOPOLD *reads:*)

LEOPOLD

"Despite the misguided opinion of Dr. Whit I can state categor-
ically that *I* was driving the car at the time and was not responsible for striking the blows that killed poor Bobby Franks. I
would only be too happy to swear under oath that *Nathan
Leopold* was responsible for the murderous attack ..."

You've got to be kidding!

LOEB

Come on, Babe—

LEOPOLD

You know perfectly well you did it—what's the use of claiming it
was me? It makes no difference as to our actual guilt. We are
both equally guilty!

LOEB

Just so. It makes no legal difference anyhow, so why do you care?

(LEOPOLD *stares at him.*)

LOEB

Look, I just think it would be easier on my Mom if she thought
you did it. Maybe if she thinks I didn't actually, you know ... kill
him ... then maybe she might ... I don't know...

LEOPOLD

I have a family too, you know!

LOEB

And your family has been with you every step of the way!

LEOPOLD

I'm sorry, Dick, I can't go along with this.

LOEB (*Angry*)
Why is this such a fucking big deal with you all of a sudden?

LEOPOLD

Does the *truth* have no value then?

LOEB

I don't see why. When did it ever before?

LEOPOLD

I am incapable of murdering anyone!

LOEB

Is that so? Nathan Leopold, Jr, the "Mad Genius" not capable of
murder? I mean, Babe, today I got this postcard from some little floozy that said: "Keep your faith up, Dick. We know that you
have been badly led astray by that *horrible Leopold*." How do
you like that, Horrible Leopold?

LEOPOLD

It's nonsense!

LOEB

Of course it is! I know that, old chum, and you know that, but
they don't know that. So we laugh at them, just like always.

(*Beat.*)

So what's it going to be then? Do we go on together or do we go our separate ways?

What do you say, boy-o? Us against us, or us against them?

LEOPOLD

I will not accept this.

LOEB

You will not accept this?

(*Beat.*)

LEOPOLD

No.

LOEB (*A sudden wrenching implosion*)

This is what they want, you know that don't you?—they want to split us up. *They want to tear us apart.*—They always have—*that's all anyone's ever wanted. But we can't let them, Babe, we can't.*

LEOPOLD

I'm sorry, Dick. No.

(Pause. Loeb moves to touch Leopold.)

LEOPOLD (*Firmly, gently*)

Please, don't touch me.

(*Beat.*)

LOEB

You're the only one I've got left, Babe. Don't leave me.

(DARROW *enters.*)

DARROW

All right, sit down, boys.

(*They sit.*)

DARROW

You've got to answer a question for me. All right?

LEOPOLD

Of course.

DARROW

Dick?

LOEB

Sure.

(*Pause.*)

DARROW

Why did you kill Bobby Franks?

(*Pause.* LOEB *finally looks away and laughs sharply.* LEOPOLD *stares at* DARROW.)

DARROW

Babe?

LEOPOLD

I don't see the point of—

DARROW

No, I want to know.

LEOPOLD

I don't want to discuss this—

DARROW

Babe, why did you kill Bobby Franks?

LEOPOLD

It was an intellectual test. A philosophical exercise.

DARROW

Ah. And you Dick?

LOEB

Like Babe said. To see if we could do it—exercising a natural superiority.

DARROW

A natural superiority...

(*He pauses and shakes his head sadly.*)

You know, boys, not a day goes by that I don't kick myself for taking this case. But then I always tell myself—I tell myself—no, no, there's some *truth* here if I can just find it. If I can just ask the right questions then it will all come out; all their fear and horror and remorse. And then it'll be *real* to me. If I just keep slugging away. And then this morning I thought, well, old man, you're shit out of time now, you've got a summation to give. So I ask you one last time. I think, now you'll talk to me. By this time, you ... trust me. But no—the same evasions—*the same goddamn lies*. Can you really think so little of me?

LOEB (*Suddenly*)

You talk to us like you think we're nuts! I don't think I'm nuts at all, do you, Babe?

DARROW

Dick, these were not the acts of sane men.

LOEB

But we're supermen, above the law. You can't judge us by the same standards—

LEOPOLD

Stop it, Dick—!

LOEB

No! Ubermensch! ... Remember?

LEOPOLD

Nietzsche's supermen would never have been caught. Our error was in the misinterpretation—

DARROW

Babe—

LEOPOLD

The philosophical ideal behind our crime was—!

DARROW

Babe!

LEOPOLD

No listen, this is the truth—

DARROW

Bullshit!
Useless bullshit! You can't go on justifying *hatred* by saying it's *philosophy!*

LEOPOLD

We have consistently supported our actions with clear—

DARROW

Babe—!

LEOPOLD

The ideal for our actions—!

DARROW (*Grabbing him*)

Babe! *Stop! Just stop!* You can save all your high-falutin' ideas because *I don't care!* Now listen, forget all the words and the philosophies and the facts and the figures—just stop *thinking* for one minute, and what do you have left?

What's there...? What keeps echoing inside you...?

It's your *heart*, Babe. It's the firm steady beat of your heart... Listen to it...listen to it. It can't fail you.

(*Beat.*)

Can it?

(*Beat.*)

LEOPOLD (*Softly, with difficulty*)
And what if my heart is wrong?

(*Beat.*)

DARROW
Then it is wrong.

(*Lights cross fade to...*)

SCENE 26

(*The courtroom. The summations to the judge.*)

CROWE
Your Honor, a closing summation in a case such as this leaves a lot of room for showy oratory. I shall leave that to the distinguished Counsel for the Defense—instead I shall appeal to your reasoning mind and your firm respect for the laws of our state. It is the position of the State that there is but one penalty that is proportional to the turpitude of this crime, only one penalty that applies to a crime of this sort, and that is death.

I suppose I should apologize for using the word "death"; I mean I'd hate to frighten these two poor, misunderstood *lads*. I wouldn't want to shock their tender ears by such a cruel reference to the penalty of death, to the laws of our state. I would never want to upset these sweet babes. Heavens no!

(*Quietly to* DARROW.)

Mr. Darrow, we are not taken in.

The defense will undoubtedly plead for mercy. *What mercy did they show Bobby Franks?* After striking two blows, from behind, they dragged him into the rear of the car, hit him again, and gouged out his life! *Mercy?* Your Honor it is an insult to come before the bar of justice and beg for mercy. I know Your Honor will be as merciful to these two defendants sitting here as they were to Bobby Franks!

Hang these heartless "supermen"! Hang them! For if we do not hang these two most brutal murderers, we might as well abolish capital punishment because it will mean nothing in the eyes of the law. And I want to say that those men who have reached the gallows prior to this time have been unjustly treated if these two do not follow!

(*Pause.*)

I submit to Your Honor, please, if we can take the power of American manhood and send them to their death in the trenches of France, we have an equal right to take the lives of these two men for violating the laws that our soldiers gave their lives to defend. Many a boy eighteen years of age lies buried beneath the bloody earth of the Somme. My brother is one of them. How can we face his memory, and the memory of all those men, and tell them that they did not die in vain if we disregard the morality and truth they died for? How can we tell them that the America they loved has come to this? To this! No, it cannot be.

Your Honor, society can endure. Criminals can escape punishment, and the law can endure. All manner of grime and corruption can be heaped on the head of pure Justice, and still she will hold her head high in pride. But if a court, such as this court, should say that it believes in the doctrine of Darrow, that you should not hang when the law says you must, then a greater blow has been struck to our institutions than by a hundred, yes, a thousand murderers. And it is a blow, Your Honor, that will leave us crippled! *Violated!* And palpably less than we were before these streets were echoing with the names of Leopold and Loeb!

Your honor, they committed the crime. They showed no mercy. They confessed to the crime. They've shown no remorse. The law tells us our duty. Give us... *justice*.

(CROWE *returns to his table. He sits.*)

(DARROW *slowly stands and walks forward. He addresses the court:*)

DARROW

Your Honor, there has never been a case in Illinois where on a plea of guilty a boy under the age of twenty-one has been sentenced to death. Yet this court is urged to hang two boys contrary to the precedents, contrary to the acts of every judge who ever held court in this state.

(*He turns to* CROWE.)

Why? Tell me the public necessity for this?

Why should a judge be urged by every argument, moderate and immoderate, to hang two boys in the face of every precedent in Illinois, and in the face of the progress of the last fifty years?

In the last six weeks I have heard nothing but a cry for blood. I have heard from the office of the State's Attorney only ugly hate. I have heard precedents quoted that would be a *disgrace to a savage race!* I have heard a court implored to hang two boys, in the face of science, in the face of philosophy, in the face of humanity, in the face of all the better and humane thoughts of the age. All in the name of *justice*.

And what is my friend's idea of justice? "Give them the same mercy they gave Bobby Franks!" He says we should strike out, blindly, just like them—drag this court down to their *insane level*. Is that justice? Is that the law? Is this what a court should do? I say no. The law can be vindicated without killing anyone else. If the state where I live is not more humane, more considerate, more kind and more intelligent than the mad act of these two boys—well, I am sorry that I have lived so long.

It might shock the state's counsel that Bobby Franks was put into a culvert and left after he was dead. But, Your Honor, I can think of an equally shocking scene. I can think of taking two boys and penning them into a cell, checking off the days and hours and minutes until they will be taken out and hanged...

(*He walks to* LEOPOLD *and* LOEB.)

I can picture them, wakened in the dim light of morning, furnished with a suit of clothes by the State, led to the scaffold, their feet tied, black hoods drawn over their heads, stood on a trap-door, the hangman pressing the spring so that it gives way under them. I can see them falling through space and stopped by the rope around their necks. I can see them swinging back and forth in the gray morning's light.

Wouldn't that be a glorious day for Chicago? Wouldn't that be a glorious triumph for the State's Attorney? *Wouldn't it be a glorious triumph for justice in this land?*

(*Pause.*)

I ask you, were these two boys in their right minds? Here were two boys with good intellect and all the prospect that life can hold out for the young. Boys with all the world before them. And they gave it up for *nothing*.

(*He spins on* LEOPOLD *and* LOEB.)

Nothing!

(*He roams, trying to figure it all out.*)

That they were reasoning and sane and sound is unthinkable! Why did they kill Bobby Franks? Not for money, not for spite, not for hate. They killed him as they might kill a spider or a fly, for the experience...

(*He stops.*)

No... No... It's even simpler than that. They killed *him because they were made that way*. Because somewhere... somehow... in the infinite processes that go into the making of a boy or a man something... *slipped*.

(DARROW *remains standing as lights cross-fade to*)

(*The jail anteroom.* LEOPOLD *and* LOEB *stand. Pause.*)

LEOPOLD

Howya doing?

LOEB

Okay.

(*Beat.*)

LEOPOLD

You sure you're alright?

LOEB

Feeling a little melancholic, I guess.

LEOPOLD

Sure.

(*Pause.*)

LOEB

So this is really it.

LEOPOLD

The summations you mean?

LOEB

Yeah.

LEOPOLD

It'll work out alright, you'll see.

LOEB

You think?

LEOPOLD

Of course.

LOEB

You really think we'll make it?

LEOPOLD

You bet.

(*Beat.*)

LOEB

You never really got the hang of the effortless lie.

LEOPOLD (*Smiling*)

Well, I'll have time to work on it.

LOEB

Let's hope.

(*Pause.*)

LOEB

Babe... do you ever...

LEOPOLD

What?

LOEB

Forget it.

LEOPOLD

Do I ever what?

LOEB

Do you ever think what might have happened if we hadn't...

LEOPOLD

If we hadn't killed Bobby Franks?

LOEB

Yes.

LEOPOLD

I do.

(*Beat.*)

LOEB

And?

(*Beat.*)

LEOPOLD

We would have been comfortable. Unexceptional.

(*Pause.*)

LOEB

They won't photograph us, will they?

LEOPOLD

When?

LOEB

If they hang us. They won't photograph us on the gallows?

LEOPOLD

Of course not.

LOEB

I wouldn't want that.

(*Pause.*)

LOEB

Will it hurt?

LEOPOLD

No, our necks will break and the spinal column will be severed. If they've done it right.

LOEB

What if they haven't?

LEOPOLD

I'm sure they know how to do it.

LOEB

But what if they make a mistake?

LEOPOLD

Then we would choke.

(*Pause.*)

LOEB

If they hang us what do you want them to do with you? With your body?

LEOPOLD

I haven't really thought about it. I suppose bury me next to my mother.

LOEB

Mm.

LEOPOLD

Maybe I'd want a bird feeder near my grave. Yes, I would like that. That would make me happy in the hereafter. If I believed in the hereafter which, of course ... I don't.
 What about you?

(*Beat.*)

LOEB

I want them to burn me. Right down to ashes. And then throw me somewhere dark. Away from everybody. I want some stranger to take me deep into the woods, in Minnesota or some-thing, and dump me where no one will ever come across me again.

(*Pause.*)

LEOPOLD

Dick, why did we kill Bobby Franks?

(*Pause. They look at each other.*)

LOEB

I don't know.

LEOPOLD (*With great difficulty*)

I don't know either.

(*Pause.*)

We're not Supermen, are we?

(*Beat.*)

LOEB

No, I guess not.

(*Lights cross fade back to...*)

DARROW

I have stood for three months as one might stand trying to sweep back the tide. I wish to make no false pretenses to this court. The easiest thing and the most popular thing to do would be to hang my clients. I know it. Men and women who do not think will applaud. The cruel and thoughtless will approve. It will be easy ... today. But stretching out over this land more and more fathers and mothers, the humane, the kind and the hopeful—who are gaining an understanding not only of these two boys, but of their own as well—they will join in no acclaim at the death of my clients. *They would ask that the shedding of blood be stopped!*

(*Pause.*)

Your Honor stands now between the future and the past. I *know* the future is with me, and what I stand for here. I am pleading for life and understanding. I am pleading for the infinite mercy that considers all. I am pleading for a time when hatred and cruelty will not control the hearts of men, when we can learn by reason and judgment and understanding that *mercy* is the highest attribute of man. And it is all that will someday ... *someday* ... redeem us.

(*Darrow returns to his table. He sits.*)

(*Lights cross fade to...*)

SCENE 27

(LEOPOLD *and* LOEB *stand downstage. A party at the University of Chicago. Their first meeting.* LEOPOLD *is initially brusque and condescending to* LOEB.)

LOEB

Leopold, right?

LEOPOLD

That's right.

LOEB

My name's Dick Loeb. Your family lives in Kenwood too, right?

LEOPOLD

On Greenwood.

LOEB

I live on Ellis!

LEOPOLD

Small world.

LOEB (*Indicating party*)

Can you believe this party?

LEOPOLD

Pretty boring.

(*Beat.*)

LOEB

So, what are you studying here?

LEOPOLD

Law... and ornithology.

LOEB

Ornithology?

                    LEOPOLD
Birds.

                    LOEB
Oh... I thought that was bugs.

                    LEOPOLD
Entomology.

                    LOEB
What?

                    LEOPOLD
The study of insects is called entomology.

                    LOEB
Oh...
     (*Beat.*)
Birds, huh?

                    LEOPOLD
Yes.

                    LOEB
What is it you like about birds?

          LEOPOLD (*With withering
            sarcasm as he moves away*)
Ohh... they seem so happy, I suppose.

                    LOEB
And predatory.

     (LEOPOLD *stops, intrigued.*)

                    LEOPOLD
And predatory.
     (*Beat. He returns to* LOEB.)

I give lectures on local ornithology. You should come sometime.

LOEB

Maybe I will, um ...

LEOPOLD

Nathan.

LOEB

Nathan.

(*Beat.*)

You play bridge?

LEOPOLD

Extremely well.

LOEB

Me too.

LEOPOLD

Especially when I cheat.

LOEB

Me too.

(*Beat.*)

LEOPOLD

We should play sometime.

LOEB

You're on.

LEOPOLD

How about now?

LOEB

Well... we need two others. How about Max and Dick Rubel—

LEOPOLD

How about we play poker?

(*Beat as* LOEB *looks at* LEOPOLD, *amused.*)

LOEB

Where?

LEOPOLD

I've got a car.

LOEB

Poker in a car?

LEOPOLD

I've got a flask in the glove compartment. We could make a night of it.

LOEB

I have to be in early.

LEOPOLD

No you don't.

(*Long pause as they stare at each other.*)

LOEB

You're on, Nathan.

LEOPOLD

Call me Babe.

LOEB

Babe.

(*Pause as they look at each other.*)

REPORTER 1

September 10th: Dickie And Babe Escape the Noose. Judge's Verdict: Life Plus Ninety-nine Years.

(*The lights fade to a cold light on* LEOPOLD *and* LOEB, *looking out. The light fades.*)